AMERICA
AT THE
THRESHOLD
OF
DESTINY

AMERICA AT THE THRESHOLD OF DESTINY

Arrow Publications
P.O. Box 10102
Cedar Rapids, IA 52410
Phone: (319) 395-7833
Fax: (319) 395-7353

CONTENTS

PREFACE

This is not so much a preface as it is an open letter to those who might think I am ignoring America's sins. By the time you have completed reading this book, I'm sure that you will have discovered why I disagree with those who are judging and condemning the United States. However, before I speak of America's future, let me familiarize you with my past.

I am not ignorant of America's sins. I have wept, probably more than most, over the sins of our nation, especially the unprincipled conduct displayed by President Clinton with Monica Lewinski. Yet, let me also say that I cried longer and harder over the decision to publish the pornographic account of his sin to the world. I moaned for weeks at the defilement of America's young children who, in public schools, had to endure this shameless testimony as required reading. I was outraged by the lack of discretion in handling the sin more than the actual immoral relationship itself.

I'm not glossing over the mystery of iniquity that seems to continually attach its tendrils around American culture. I am troubled when I hear of Christians, especially pastors, who think nothing of watching movies where sex, violence and foul language are part of the "entertainment." I don't feel prudish at all when I say that I am offended by the sexually blatant magazine covers at checkout counters. I hate dirty jokes; crude humor is an offense to me.

I despise racial jokes and ethnic slurs. In fact, I am ashamed before God for the history of poor race relations in America and that we have taken so long to begin to make things right. This is a charge against us in heaven for which I have positioned myself in ongoing prayer and repentance before God.

I don't want you to think that I am unburdened or ignoring the wholesale cheapening of life in America, whether it manifests through abortion or with gangs or with child abuse or wife beating or when any murder occurs. I'm not aloof from these things, not in the least. I have fasted over them, prayed about them, wept concerning them and been, at times, sick because of them. I know that it was largely because of mankind's violence that God destroyed the world during Noah's day, so I am deeply aware of these things.

When homosexual agendas, witchcraft, New Age cults, "Christian" cults, atheism or paganism are promoted in America for any reason, it disturbs me greatly. When I see my tax money misspent in Washington on pork roll projects, while hundreds of thousands of children struggle to rise above the horror of inner city survival, my soul burns within me.

Let me also say that I am deeply grieved over the sins of the church: the divisions, ambitions, slanders, immoralities, prayerlessness and worldliness. I lament that, more often than not, the church has not been an example to the world of righteousness and true holiness.

Indeed, there are many things that have distressed me about American culture. So, if you are concerned about sin in this nation, I want you to know that I am as well. We are united together and in agreement concerning the reality of sin and its potential consequences in our culture.

Yet, I have not just been "vexed" like Lot about the sins I witnessed; I have been involved in trying to change them. In the past, I have been arrested for protesting against abortion (together with my two oldest children).

I have published pro-life letters to newspaper editors and pleaded directly with pro-choice leaders.

Concerning race relations, long before it became a pattern, I organized a regional reconciliation service between blacks and whites at our city hall. I brought together news reporters and television crews, mayors, police chiefs and church and community leaders from various backgrounds and cultures. I personally paid for it all. I've been hosting similar reconciliation services throughout scores of cities in North America.

Concerning the church, I doubt that there are many who have done more to unite Christians than me. According to the Lord's prayer for oneness among His people (see John 17:20–21), in hundreds of cities with thousands of pastors, I have led citywide meetings with no other goal than to humble ourselves in repentance and prayer.

I'm not telling you this to boast, but to assure you that what I have to say about America's future is not being written by someone far removed from these pressing issues. Along with you, I believe the church needs to confront sin and injustice, speaking the truth in love to those in bondage to sin.

However, throughout my struggle I have not only been made aware of America's sinfulness, I have simultaneously been discovering something about the Almighty. What I have found is not just theological information, it's *revelation* concerning God's heart: the Lord is good. He is slow to anger and abundant in lovingkindness; He has shown that He will relent concerning calamity, even if there is only one person praying for mercy. This is what I pray you will understand by the time you have completed this book.

That's why I'm not condemning America or accusing the President or calling for divine wrath to fall on this nation. I am not condemning America because Jesus is not condemning it! Yes, He is condemning the sin, but *the Lord is not looking for an opportunity to destroy us; He is seeking opportunities to forgive and restore us.*

Attaining an accurate knowledge of America's sins does nothing to remedy them. But for all that is wrong in America, the sins of self-righteousness, pride, and carnal judging are, to me, perhaps the most grievous. For in those sins, we misrepresent the heart and nature of Christ.

My dear friends, if we will indeed seek to be uncompromising with sin, let us start with ourselves and let us deal with these sins of pride and anger. For I believe that if we will repent of self-righteousness, and return to our holy quest to reveal the redemptive, intercessory nature of Christ, revival will surely come, first to the church and then to the world around us. Yes, I am fully and passionately convinced, when Christ is revealed through His people, mercy will triumph over judgment.

INTRODUCTION

I never intended to write this book. In fact, I was working on several other projects that seemed more pressing to me than this. However, as I came in contact with an increasing number of angry, bitter Christians—individuals who were predicting the destruction of America—I realized a spirit other than Christ's was infiltrating the church.

The Lord's corrective judgments are wholesome, even if painful; however, these voices were not calling merely for God to correct, but to destroy. I thought, "This cannot be happening, not now." The prayer movement was expanding, reconciliation between churches, cultures and denominations was increasing. We had the "Stand in the Gap" prayer summit in Washington, D.C., and we were seeing so many breakthroughs and evidences in our society, empirical evidence, that God was answering our prayers.

Perhaps what bothered me most was I saw people who had been praying, now silenced and discouraged. I could see from their wilted spirits that their hope had been stolen. Indeed, if God was definitely going to destroy America, why pray? Why fast? Many others were deeply troubled by fears and concerns for their loved ones. A few had actually stopped praying for revival and had joined the angry voices calling the Almighty to judge America.

The Bible says that without a vision, people perish (Prov 29:18). We were being seduced by a spirit of hopelessness, which was descending and spreading upon God's people like a thick, dark mist.

The Holy Spirit reminded me of Israel, encamped on the plains of Moab. The Hebrews were about to enter the Promised Land after spending nearly forty years in the wilderness. God had done a tremendous work transforming these former slaves into a mighty army. To counter the advancing Hebrews, Balak, a Moabite king, hired the soothsayer Balaam to curse Israel. However, each time Balaam opened his mouth to utter his curse, God gave him blessings to speak instead. In fact, some of the most encouraging words in the Bible were spoken by a man who was actually trying to curse God's people!

There was nothing the powers of darkness could do to stop the people whom God had blessed. Then Balaam had an idea. He convinced Balak that, if Israel could be tempted to sin, God Himself would judge them. So Balaam counseled that the Midianite and Moabite women should seduce the Israelite men. Balaam's plan worked and the Lord sent a terrible plague into Israel which killed 24,000 men (Num 25; 31:16).

As Christians, we are not as advanced toward our goals as the Israelites were toward theirs—we are not yet encamped on the plains of a national awakening—but the principle is the same: If we can be seduced to turn from redemptive intercessory prayer, which has brought significant changes to the body of Christ and blessing to America, and we return to our old judgmental, self-righteous ways, then God will be forced to judge us as harshly as we have been judging others.

So, at the onset, my goal has been to defend the mercy path upon which the Lord has been leading the church these past years. Yet, as I have sought the Lord, I felt the burning witness of God's Holy Spirit saying that there are many aspects of this nation that are still precious to God. I beheld that the prayer movement in the nation has had a very positive effect in many areas of American society.

Because of prayer, America is actually moving again toward its destiny and away from judgment.

There are insights that I will write about concerning the United States that I have not heard taught before. Please keep my views in context with what others are saying, especially heeding what the Lord may be saying to your local area. Listen prayerfully, but not fearfully, to those who warn of dangers ahead. However, if a warning does not offer hope, do not drink deeply from its spirit. Remember always: grace and truth are realized in Jesus Christ. If a "word" comes only with condemnation and without grace, vision and hope, it is not the Spirit of Jesus Christ, but the accuser.

Because we have focused so intensely on removing the negative traits in this nation, we have become more vulnerable to noticing the "half empty" glass of America's righteousness. I seek to emphasize that the glass is "half full" and increasing. I will speak about what others have overlooked. God has shed many graces on our land and I will bring to remembrance a few.

I know many are looking for a "crystal ball" to tell them the future: What about Y2K? What will happen with the economy? Will there be war? On and on the list unfolds. It is my contention that God will not give us a "crystal ball"; He does not want us wondering about the future. He bids us to *create* it through the knowledge of His Word and the power of intercession. Did not Jesus Himself teach us to pray, "Thy kingdom come, Thy will be done on earth, as it is in heaven"? Christ calls us to stop wondering and start believing. All things are possible to those who believe. We can have the kingdom of heaven in America, healing and restoring our cities, if we will overcome the spirit of hopelessness and unbelief. Even if a prophecy of wrath seems accurate, remember: redemptive prayer is more powerful than prophecy.

My only regret is that there was so much to present. I forced myself to pare back this text to two essential themes: prayer and the destiny of the U.S. I wanted to talk about biblical principles and patterns of judgment, when the Almighty releases His wrath and why He does so. I also have a number of chapters on how to communicate the genuine passions of our prophetic impulses without losing balance and perspective or becoming presumptuous. There were additional chapters about this amazing harvest season in which we find ourselves today, and several more chapters about prayer and the destiny of America. These will all have to wait for another time, although some may be published on our web site: http://www.frangipane.org.

Because this book is dated somewhat by references to Bill Clinton, Y2K, finances and current world conditions, in the future I may republish it under a different title with a focus purely on prayer and Christlikeness.

One last thought. If I sound overly aggressive in my approach to eliminating judgmentalism from the church, please forgive me. God has great plans for the church and America; I am simply seeking to defend them.

This book is dedicated to the millions of people worldwide who love America and are, even now, crying out to God for His mercy.

PART ONE:

THE CHURCH IN THE IMAGE OF CHRIST

*But we all, with unveiled face beholding
as in a mirror the glory of the Lord,
are being transformed into the same image
from glory to glory,
just as from the Lord, the Spirit.*

—2 Cor 3:18—

CHAPTER ONE

A WORLD
WITHOUT AMERICA

Recently, a number of respected church leaders, frustrated with America's slow turn to repentance, have proclaimed that divine wrath is coming to our land. "If God does not destroy America," one influential pastor wrote, "He will have to repent to Sodom and Gomorrah."

Certainly, there are many things morally wrong with America, but America is not Sodom or Gomorrah. Neither is it a re-emergence of the spirit of ancient Babylon. You will not find charged against this land the "blood of prophets and of saints and of all who have been slain on the earth" (Rev 18:24). The spiritual influence of these archetypes is here, just as they are also manifested throughout the world, but America is much more than the sum of its sins and failures.

America does not answer to any singular prophetic profile. It is not the Promised Land, but it *is* a land of promise. For those who predict the decline and fall of this nation, I'm sorry to disappoint you: America has only just begun to rise. Indeed, as we enter the 21ˢᵗ century, I believe we will find this nation, imperfect as it is, increasing its global influence.

It is easy to call for, predict, and then anticipate the manifestation of divine wrath. It plays perfectly into our fears. Once you adjust your perception to expect doom, religious zeal supplies all sorts of apocalyptic visions of the end. The problem is, visions born of fear are not synonymous with visions born of God.

For more than thirty years I have heard scores of "doom and destruction" predictions that were going to be fulfilled by a certain date. We were supposed to all die in nuclear war in 1979; we were to be raptured in 1988 (then 1989, when '88 did not come to pass); then the Gulf War would turn into Armageddon; and, of course in 1998, fifty years after Israel's birth, the Lord was sure to return.

Shall I go on? I cannot remember one prophecy that has been even remotely fulfilled. The fact is, instead of destroying the world, the Lord has raised up what may be the most expansive prayer movement in generations (if not in all of time). He has been reconciling and uniting His church (for the first time in its history), revival is beginning in a number of places, and converts by the *hundreds of millions* (that is not a misprint) have come to Christ worldwide during this same period! People thought the world was going to disintegrate; instead, we have entered the greatest season of harvest in the history of the church!

Why did those predictions of wrath fall to the ground unfulfilled? Maybe there are many reasons, but the plain, obvious truth is that God is more patient and merciful than we previously imagined. In fact, I believe that, at least in the next few years, the Lord has something else planned for America other than destruction.

Judging Prophecy

The Lord spoke about discerning the origin of prophetic words in the book of Deuteronomy. He said,

"And you may say in your heart, 'How shall we know the word which the Lord has not spoken?'

"When a prophet speaks in the name of the Lord, if the thing does not come about or come true, that is the thing which the Lord has not spoken. The prophet has spoken it presumptuously; you shall not be afraid of him."   —Deut 18:21–22

God's Word plainly says, "If the thing does not come about . . . the Lord has not spoken."

We all make mistakes. Sometimes we are moved by fears to make presumptuous predictions. A person is not a false prophet because he makes a mistake. The Lord does not condemn me and neither am I condemning anyone. But we need to admit when we are wrong and examine why our predictions fell to the ground.

In the New Testament Paul instructs the church, "Let two or three prophets speak, and let the others pass judgment. But if a revelation is made to another who is seated, let the first keep silent" (1 Cor 14:29–30).

So, we've heard the potential for divine wrath, but now it is time to balance the message of judgment with vision and mercy. It is time for some who have been seated to share their revelation. You be the judge.

Before we continue, however, let me clarify two things. One, if you are trapped in habitual sin, you *should* fear. There is only one antidote to this fear and that is to repent and get right with God. The second clarification is this: Until the transformation of our mortal bodies, the

Lord's *corrective* judgments will be with us always. Those whom He loves He reproves and disciplines. It is good that God judges what is wrong in us. May He never stop judging the sin in me or in the church or in America. There will always be consequences for our actions.

But let me assure you, there is a difference between God's *corrective* judgments and the manifestation of His wrath. Corrective judgment is guided by His mercy. Wrath is the venting of His anger. It is not in the Lord's heart to destroy this nation; humble and then heal, yes, but not destroy.

My passion is to inspire the church to see America the way a loving parent views an unbroken teenager, which is how I believe God sees this land. He is not ready to destroy us. In truth, He is patiently working His will. He will fulfill what He has begun with this land. Let us not become impatient as we wait for His fulfillment. The very least the Lord wants to do with America is use it to keep the world open for harvest. For that reason alone we must stand in continued intercession for our country. Yet, if we possess no clear vision for the United States, may the Lord reveal His passion for mercy even when we are convinced He is warning of wrath.

IF THE NAZIS HAD WON WWII

To help give us perspective on Christ's view of America, let's imagine what civilization would be like today *without* the United States. Let's step back in time and consider where the world would be if the leading Axis powers, Germany and Japan, had defeated the Allies in WWII.

To make this "alternate reality" credible, let's weave into our imaginary world some facts about America as it was in the 1930s. Prior to WWII, much of America was in serious moral decline. The moral restraints of the Victorian Era had evaporated in the heat of the "Roaring Twenties." A tremendous upswing of organized crime brought gang violence, extortion and corruption, which infiltrated huge segments of society and government. Racial injustice toward blacks was rampant, and prejudice against the more recent immigrants, the Irish, Italians, Asians and Jews was a way of life.

Then, in 1933, the singular redeeming virtue of the times, Prohibition, was repealed. It passed by a national vote of almost 75%. Literally overnight, America went from outlawing alcoholic beverages to drunken celebrations in the streets.

These were the facts concerning America in the '20s and '30s. America suffered the consequences of its sins as the Great Depression lingered and worsened, but God had no intention of destroying this land. The Lord knew that all hell was marshaling forces in Germany and Japan; America, sinful as it was, was vital to the defense of God's plan.

But imagine if frustrated church leaders in the '30s had begun to ask God to judge the U.S. for its sins. And suppose He actually did what these short-sighted leaders asked: He allowed the Great Depression to crumble into anarchy and civil war, which, as a result, fractured the U.S. into three regional sub-countries: the North, South and West.

So, in our imaginary world, the year is 1939. Because God has answered the prayer of angry Christians, America does not exist. Then World War II explodes. By 1942, the tidal wave of German military power has advanced and conquered all its surrounding nations. In 1943, England falls. Almost at the same time, Africa too bows beneath the shadow of the Swastika.

Then, as 1945 begins, the Nazis secretly test their first atomic bombs; two months later, they unleash them upon sixteen Russian cities. Twenty-five million people die in the atomic blast and, with them, mankind's hope of resisting the Third Reich is also destroyed.

In the Far East, meanwhile, no nation was strong enough to match the fierce, unrelenting might of the Japanese. The Imperial Army crushed and pillaged both China and Korea. It rolled southwestward and overwhelmed India and Pakistan, making surrogate armies of their vast multitudes. They then fulfilled their blood lust upon southeast Asia and Australia.

By 1946, the empire of the Rising Sun had ascended over Asia to the Hawaiian Islands; Japan's western boundaries extended to Pakistan and central Russia. The Third Reich ruled everywhere else. Throughout the world, a grid of satanic control had locked in place, securing the spiritual realms over the earth in impenetrable darkness.

THE CONSEQUENCES

It is not hard to imagine the above scenario or something like it if, in the '30s, the balance of power in the world was void of the United States. Obviously, thankfully, in spite of its sins, God did not destroy America. Instead, He healed our nation and actually made it stronger!

But let's carry our journey into today's time frame. Yes, we do have problems in our world, but what would civilization be like if the concept of a Free World had died during World War II?

The United States is reunited, but it is ruled by Nazi Germany and policed by German SS troops and Gestapo. In this world without American influence, democracy is not to be found anywhere on earth. The world we live in is a totalitarian society: it is void of freedom.

Mein Kampf, Hitler's life story, is taught and applied in every level of academia; his racist ideologies are enforced and framed in America's new Constitution. Adolf Hitler has not just replaced George Washington as our founding father, he has pronounced himself "savior of the world." Even our calendars have been reset. The first year of the New Order of the Third Reich coincides with Hitler's birth year. American children enter schools singing hymns to the Fuhrer; each child is without deformity, for children with birth defects do not live beyond their first week.

Americans have been trained to believe that this new world, having been cleansed of Jews, Gypsies and other so-called "undesirables," has evolved into a purer form of humanity. German-controlled "social engineering" has assigned values to races; except for the Japanese, all non-whites are classified as "servant races."

All liberty is gone. There exists no freedom of press or right of protest. There is no balance of power in government, no political parties, no open debate and no forums of ideas. There is a state church, but freedom of religion is no longer a civil right. There exists no open, vibrant evangelical Christian community. Pentecostalism is considered a mental disorder and those who practice spiritual gifts are institutionalized. Though there might, indeed, be a true, underground church, attendance is at the risk of one's life. There are no evangelical books, no contemporary Christian music, no spiritual media resources. The last five popes are German-born and "Billy Graham" is a fairly common but insignificant name.

Certainly, one of the worst consequences would exist in the Middle East: There would be no Israel. In fact, except for those few surviving Jews hiding in the remote recesses of the earth, a world without America would be a world without Jews.

Yet, beyond all this, the most tragic reality is that, since WWII, the expansion of evangelical Christianity has virtually ceased. Instead of the nearly half billion souls that, worldwide, have entered the kingdom of God since 1946, the apostasy has reached its full zenith.

The fact is, in spite of what is wrong and sinful in America, without its role as the leader of the free world, there would be no harvest today. Indeed, there would be great and incurable heartache on earth and much less joy in heaven in a world without America.

CHAPTER TWO

MERCY TRIUMPHS OVER JUDGMENT

Today, multitudes of fine "Bible-believing" Christians think nothing of venting their anger and bitterness toward America and its sins. Understandably, there has been much to grieve over. We *should* be deeply troubled, like Lot, with the "conduct of unprincipled men" (2 Pet 2:7). We should at least be moved to tears and prayer, if not anointed action.

Yet, the moment we think our warfare is "against flesh and blood," or begin to call for divine wrath against people, we step outside the will of God. Indeed, when Jesus' disciples asked for fire to fall on the Samaritans, He told them plainly, "You do not know what kind of spirit you are of" (Luke 9:55).

This is exactly our problem: *Church people do not know the difference between a judgmental spirit and the Spirit of Christ, the Redeemer.* Indeed, we are not sent as Old Testament prophets, calling fire and judgment down on sinners.

Although America is guilty of many sins, only One is worthy to break the seals and open the book of God's wrath: the slain Lamb standing at God's throne (see Rev 5). Until He opens the book, we must pray for mercy; until we become lamb-like, our judging is misguided.

This does not mean we should minimize the wantonness that has spread through our society into the world. Sin cannot be glossed over or ignored. Yet, it is precisely *because* sin is utterly vile that we must embrace our role to stand before God in intercession.

Intercession is the essence of the life of Christ. Jesus beheld the depravity of mankind's sin. He did not excuse it. He examined it carefully, and then took the form of a man and died for it. He calls us to pattern our lives after His. Indeed, we are not minimizing sin when we maximize Christ's mercy. We are not white-washing sin; we are blood-washing it.

James tells us, "mercy triumphs over judgment" (James 2:13). To live the life of mercy plays perfectly into God's heart. Mercy precisely fulfills the divine purpose: to transform man into the Redeemer's image.

Throughout His life, Jesus reached out to people who were left out. He loved those whom others despised and excluded. Yet, His practice of dining with sinners offended the Pharisees and they confronted Jesus' disciples.

"Why is your Teacher eating with the tax-gatherers and sinners?" (Matt 9:11)

When Jesus heard the question, He answered, "It is not those who are healthy who need a physician, but those who are sick. But go and learn what this means, 'I desire compassion, and not sacrifice,' for I did not come to call the righteous, but sinners" (Matt 9:12–13).

He told the self-righteous to go and learn what God meant when He said, "I desire compassion (mercy), and

not sacrifice." A religion without love is an abomination
to God.

THE HOUSE OF PRAYER

Jesus said His Father's house would be a "house of
prayer for all the nations" (Mark 11:17). True prayer is
born of love and comes in the *midst* of sin and need. It
comes not to condemn, but to cover. All nations sin. All
cultures have crises. Yet, these times can become turning
points if, in the time of distress, intercessors cry to God for
mercy. Thus, prayer brings redemption from disaster.

The church is created, not to fulfill God's wrath, but
to complete His mercy. Remember, we are called to be a
house of prayer *for* all nations. Consider passionately this
phrase: "prayer for." Jesus taught, "pray for" those who
persecute and mistreat you. Paul tells us that God desires
all men to be saved. Therefore, he urges that "entreaties
and prayers . . . be made on behalf of all men, for kings
and all who are in authority" (1 Tim 2:1–2). When Job
"prayed for" his friends, God fully restored him (Job 42).
We are to "pray for" the peace of Jerusalem (Ps 122:6),
and "pray for" each other, that we may be healed (James
5:16).

"But," you argue, "America is a modern manifestation
of ancient Babylon." No, it is not! But even if it was, when
the Lord exiled Israel to Babylon, He said, "Seek the
welfare of the city where I have sent you . . . and pray to
the Lord on its behalf; for in its welfare you will have
welfare" (Jer 29:7).

Over and over again the command is to pray *for*, not
against; not vindictively, but mercifully; not condemn-
ingly, but compassionately, appealing to God to bring

forgiveness and redemption. The problem is that too many Christians have become disciples of CNN and *TIME* rather than followers of Jesus Christ. We think conforming to our political party is the same as attaining the standards of God. It is not.

Study Isaiah 53. It reveals in wondrous detail the Savior's nature: Christ numbered Himself *with* sinners. He interceded *for* transgressors. He is "with" us and "for" us, even when He must reveal to us our iniquity.

But the world sees a church with rocks in its hands looking for adulterers and sinners. We have become the "church of the angry Christians." In the drama that is unfolding in America today, we have not been playing the role of Christ, but rather the part of the Pharisees. Let us drop the rocks from our hands, then lift our hands, without wrath, in prayer to God (1 Tim 2:8).

PRAYER FOR THE PRESIDENT

God does not want us to be judgmental; He wants us prayer-mental. As instinctively as we judge people, we should pray for them instead. Today, countless Christians are angry with their elected officials. We say our anger is "righteous indignation." Really? Jesus expressed "righteous indignation" for, perhaps, three to four hours during His ministry. Once was for the hardness of people's hearts, and the other two times were at the temple when the Father's house was used for something other than redemptive prayer (Mark 11:17). How long has your anger lasted? Are you sure your love has not grown cold; are you sure you are not seeking to justify a root of bitterness?

"Well," some argue, "the President has sinned." When Paul called for prayer for kings in 1 Timothy 2, Nero was emperor of Rome. Nero was one of the most corrupt men that ever lived. He did not have a "secret affair," he had public orgies. At night he illuminated his banquets with living torches–Christians, who were tarred and then set ablaze on poles while Nero and his guests dined! Yet, Paul wrote, "Pray for kings and all who are in authority."

Some may misread my words, assuming I think there is nothing wrong in the White House or in our society. My concern is not as much with the White House as with the Lord's house! If you are not praying for the President, the least you can do is to stop cursing him. As it is written, "You shall not speak evil of a ruler of your people" (Acts 23:5). The Father's house is a house of prayer for kings and all in authority. It must also become a source of redemptive prayer for imperfect presidents who sin.

I can understand the reason for anger toward the President in thinking he is not doing his job. But by not praying for him, you are not doing your job. In your anger, you call for God to judge America. My friend, when judgment comes, it begins "with the household of God" (1 Pet 4:17). To pray for God to judge America for its sins actually initiates judgment on the church for *its* sins! And God will start with you, and He will judge you by your standard of judgment.

When I pray for the President, I ask the Lord to protect him from the influence of ungodly counsel. Where Clinton has failed, I appeal to God to forgive him, especially for his views concerning abortion and late-term abortion. Yet, he has good things in his heart for which I thank God. He is a supporter of Israel; he cares for issues concerning people of color and the poor. Recently, he signed the "Child Online Protection Act" to help keep children from access to Internet pornography. I thank God for these things. Has he done everything perfectly? No, but neither have we.

IN THE G–A–P

I believe Jesus Christ is reaching to Bill Clinton like never before. If we pray correctly, we can see a divine transformation come both to this man and to our nation.

So many Scriptures compel us to prayer that we should not need any further encouragement to do so. Yet, let me share an experience I had concerning intercession for Mr. Clinton.

In December of 1998, family matters took me to Davenport in Scott County, Iowa. As I entered the city, I was listening to a teaching on tape and had just heard, "We need to stand in the gap for President Clinton." Immediately, a car pulled in front of me from the left lane. Next to the three numbers on its license plate were the letters G–A–P. Below the word "GAP" was the name of a county north of Scott where the plate was issued: Clinton.

If that was not enough, three seconds later, a pickup truck passed me on the right and pulled alongside the car in front. It too was from Clinton County. Unbelievably, next to its numbers were the same three letters, G–A–P.

Within no more than 30 seconds, as I heard the words, "stand in the gap for President Clinton," two vehicles appeared with exactly the same words on their plates: GAP–Clinton!

The Bible tells us that "every word will be confirmed by two or three witnesses." I know that this renewed prayer focus is not just a "fresh teaching"; to me, it is a revealed word from God, confirmed by the Holy Spirit through three witnesses.

The Lord desires us to stand in the gap, positioning ourselves between the failings of man and the sufficiency and forgiveness of God. Then, He calls us to persevere in this intercession until full transformation comes.

For all who are embittered with Bill Clinton, remember: Each of us must give an account for our sins at the judgment seat of Christ (2 Cor 5:10). Let us consider with holy fear the warning of God: "judgment will be merciless to one who has shown no mercy; mercy triumphs over judgment" (James 2:13).

Let's pray: *Father, I ask You to forgive me for my unforgiveness toward the President. Lord, I ask You to forgive, cleanse and renew him in Your mighty Presence. Appear to him, Lord, in the night hours; save him from the lies and plans of hell. Touch and heal his family and renew them as well in Your love. Lord, I ask You to forgive my harshness toward all who have offended me. Oh God, this day deliver me from my judgmental attitudes! Help me to remember in all things and at all times that mercy triumphs over judgment! Amen.*

CHAPTER THREE

WHAT
ARE YOU
BECOMING?

And when day came, He called His disciples to Him; and chose twelve of them, whom He also named as apostles: Simon, whom He also named Peter, and Andrew his brother; and James and John; and Philip and Bartholomew; and Matthew and Thomas; James the son of Alphaeus, and Simon who was called the Zealot; Judas the son of James, and Judas Iscariot, who became a traitor.   —Luke 6:13–16

J udas Iscariot had traveled both with Jesus and His disciples. Along with the others, Judas had been used mightily to "heal the sick, raise the dead, cleanse the lepers [and] cast out demons" (Matt 10:8). He knew the excitement, joy and power of walking with Jesus. Judas was numbered among the original twelve.

Yet, Judas had a serious character flaw, a moral weakness. The Scripture reveals that, despite the fact that

God was using him, Judas "was a thief, and as he had the money box, he used to pilfer what was put into it" (John 12:6).

It is significant, my friend, that Jesus allowed a thief to carry the money box. Sometimes we think the Lord is going to challenge us on every issue, but there are times when His *silence* about our repeated sin is His rebuke. Judas knew what he was doing was wrong, but since Jesus didn't directly confront him, he minimized the severity of his iniquity. Perhaps he rationalized that, if pilfering was truly bad, God would not still use him to work miracles.

How a little leaven leavens the whole lump! A relatively minor sin that we do not attend to can lead to a major sin that destroys our lives. Judas "became a traitor." He started out in ministry loyal to Jesus, but then began lying about the finances until his deceitful exterior completely hid a very corrupt interior. Judas was a thief who became a traitor, eventually taking his own life. His unrepentant compromise went from bad to worse and it destroyed him.

Today, Christians look at the world and see injustice, immorality, and corruption. The anger we feel because of these things is not only understandable, it's justified. Why shouldn't we be angry at what we see? Indeed, in many instances we are actually watching hell manifest itself through people and situations in the world!

Knowing we would grieve over the evil in the world, God's Word tells us, "Be angry, and yet do not sin" (Eph 4:26). We must discern at what point anger festers into sin. Paul continues, "do not let the sun go down on your anger."

We can be legitimately angry about things that are truly wrong, but by sundown our indignation must find a more noble, redemptive attitude of expression. We must reach for forgiveness, intercessory prayer, and a love that covers a multitude of sins. Otherwise, Paul warned, we will "give the devil an opportunity" (Eph 4:27). What happens when we do not allow the Holy Spirit to transform our frustrations? Self-righteousness begins to manifest in our souls. We become embittered and judgmental. We become cynics. The definition of a cynic is "a habitual doubter." Do you know any Christians who are cynical?

The worst thing that happens when we turn angry and cease praying is that we, like Judas, betray Christ. How? When we disown Christ's mission of intercession, redemption, and forgiveness, we turn our backs on sinners destined to hell.

Judas mutated from an apostle into a person he never intended: he *became* a traitor. Our anger, left unattended, will do the same to us. It causes us to degenerate into something we never planned on becoming: "Christian Pharisees." By allowing self-righteousness and judgmentalism to grow in the soil of unrepentant anger, we become *worse* in God's eyes than the evil which offended us.

Today, America is overstocked with angry Christians. What can we do? We must turn indignation into intercession. We must make our heartache work for us, aligning ourselves with Christ in the prayer of redemption. Otherwise, we betray Christ's purpose with our anger.

"IT'S THE PRINCIPLE"

I know Christians who refuse to surrender their anger to God concerning President Clinton. They are still offended that he was not removed from office. These are folks who love the country, possess high morals and seek to walk in integrity, yet feel perfectly justified being embittered with the President! Under the guise, "it's the principle," they feel completely unalarmed by their unchristlike attitudes.

Where in the Bible does God permit Christians to hold hatred and unforgiveness against anyone? When was it that God gave permission to Jesus' followers to remain angry towards a person for months, or even years?

Thank God, Jesus didn't look down from the cross at the Pharisees and say, "You need to be taught a lesson. I love you, but it's the principle." No. He prayed, "Father, forgive them." And then, amazingly, He *covered* their sin, saying, "They know not what they do."

The sense of Christian indignation infiltrating the church has not come from heaven. James clearly tells us that "the anger of man does not achieve the righteousness of God" (James 1:20). Don't dismiss your anger as a little sin; it disqualified Moses from entering the Promised Land!

It's time to deal with the indignation and unforgiveness. It is a terrible witness to the non-Christian world. You see, even though the unsaved don't know much about the Scriptures, they still possess a God-given sense of who Christ is when it comes to real life issues. Before they will join a church, they are watching how Christians deal with imperfect people.

There are things at stake that are bigger than our indignation about right and wrong. The world is watching how we relate to those who are morally *wrong,* even when we are biblically *right.* And they are watching to see if we look and sound like the Savior or like the Pharisees.

Yet, there is one thing more crucial than how the world sees us, and that is how Christ sees us. He is watching what is happening to our hearts. He asks each of us a simple question: Do you know what you're becoming?

Lord Jesus, help me! When did I switch from loving to judging? When did I replace the glow, the smile, of Your love with this unceasing, angry frown? Master, like Judas, I have become what I never set out to be: a traitor to Your redemptive purpose. Forgive me. Cleanse me of my anger and pride. Restore my heart until I love as You have loved me, until I stand for others in their need as You have stood for me in mine. For Your glory. Amen.

CHAPTER FOUR

ONE MAN

L et's look again at the criticism America has been receiving. A number of Christians have been saying, "If God doesn't destroy America, He will have to repent to Sodom and Gomorrah." If we are going to compare the United States to Sodom, then the church should be compared to Abraham. If we take their premise to its conclusion, we will have to add, "If the Lord does not rebuke judgmental Christians, He will have to repent to Abraham!"

What am I talking about? I am referring to the fact that when Abraham was confronted with the imminent possibility of Sodom's destruction, he did not jump on the "Destroy Sodom" bandwagon; instead, he went before the Lord and prayed for mercy for the city.

Abraham's prayer is an amazing study on the affect a mercy-motivated intercessor has on the heart of God. It tells us that the Lord is actually looking for a spark of hope, a mercy reason, to justify delaying His wrath.

Let's examine how the Lord responded to the sin of Sodom. First, He showed Abraham, His servant, what He was about to do. Why? Because God desired Abraham to intercede. When the Lord informed His servant of what was wrong in the world, it was not so he could judge it, but so that he would intercede for mercy. Remember, God *delights* in mercy and takes no pleasure in the death of the wicked (Micah 7:18, Ezek 33:11). The Lord *always* seeks for opportunities of mercy.

Therefore, let's take note of how Abraham approached the Almighty:

> Then the men turned away from there and went toward Sodom, while Abraham was still standing before the Lord. And Abraham came near and said, "Wilt Thou indeed sweep away the righteous with the wicked? Suppose there are fifty righteous within the city; wilt Thou indeed sweep it away and not spare the place for the sake of the fifty righteous who are in it?
>
> "Far be it from Thee to do such a thing, to slay the righteous with the wicked, so that the righteous and the wicked are treated alike. Far be it from Thee! Shall not the Judge of all the earth deal justly?" —Gen 18:22–25

Notice, Abraham did not pray from a place of anger. He never said, "God, it's about time You killed the perverts." Somehow, we have come to believe that noncompromising Christians must also be angry. Abraham never compromised with Sodom's depraved culture, yet he was above fleshly reaction. In fact, throughout his prayer, Abraham did not even remind the Lord of what was wrong in Sodom. He appealed, instead, to the mercy and integrity of the Lord.

This is vitally important for us, because Jesus said, "If you are Abraham's children, do the deeds of Abraham" (John 8:39). One of Abraham's most noteworthy deeds involved his intercessory prayer for Sodom, the most perverse city in the world!

Abraham first acknowledged the Lord's integrity, then he spoke to the Lord's mercy.

> "Suppose there are fifty righteous within the city;
> wilt Thou indeed sweep it away and not spare the
> place for the sake of the fifty . . ."

The Lord knew that it would be unjust to slay the righteous with the wicked; Abraham's prayer did not enlighten the Lord of some unknown fact. But the nature of life on earth is this: *God works with man to establish the future and, in the process of determining reality, He always prepares a merciful alternative.* In other words, urgent, redemptive prayer shoots straight through the mercy door to God's heart. This door is never shut, especially since we have a High Priest, Jesus Christ, ministering at the mercy seat in the heavenlies. It is open any time and every time we pray. Listen to how the Lord answered Abraham's prayer for mercy:

> "If I find in Sodom fifty righteous within the city, then
> I will spare the whole place on their account" (Gen 18:26).

How the truth of God's mercy flies in the face of those so eager to judge America! Incredibly, the Lord said He would spare the whole of Sodom if He found fifty righteous people there. Now, keep this in mind, the Hebrew word for *spare* means more than "not destroy," it also means "to forgive or pardon."

This is a tremendous revelation about the Living God: *He will minimize, delay, or even cancel a day of reckoning as long as Christ-inspired prayer is being offered for sinners!*

Time and again throughout the Scriptures the Lord proclaims an ever-present truth about His nature: He is "slow to anger, and abounding in lovingkindness" (Ex 34:6). Do we believe this? Here it is, demonstrated right in the sacred Scriptures. He tells us plainly that a few righteous people scattered in a city can preserve that city from divine wrath.

Abraham knew the love of God. They were intimate friends. Abraham, in truth, had a clear view into the heart of God based on his own experience. This interceding prophet had seen the Almighty bless, prosper, and forgive him; he pressed God's mercy toward its limits:

"What if there are forty?"

The Lord would spare it for forty.

Abraham bargained, "thirty?"

He would spare it for thirty.

"Twenty?"

He finally secured the Lord's promise not to destroy the city if he could find just ten righteous people there. Think about this, for herein we discover the heart of God: *The Lord would spare sinful Sodom for the sake of ten godly people who dwelt within it!*

HOW ABOUT YOUR COMMUNITY?

Now, let's think of your city: Are there ten good folk among you? Consider your state: Do you think there might be one thousand praying people living within its borders, people who are pleading with God for mercy? What about nationwide? Do you suppose there might be fifty thousand people interceding for America? God said He would spare Sodom for ten righteous people. Do you think God would spare the nation for the fifty thousand righteous? What if there were one and a half million men in Washington, D.C., interceding for America? Do you think God would spare this nation?

I live in a metropolitan area that has about two hundred thousand people. I can list by name scores of individuals: pastors, intercessors, youth workers, black folks, white folks, Hispanic folks, native Americans, Asian Americans, Christian business people, moms, dads, godly teenagers, praying grandmothers, secretaries, righteous policemen and on and on—far more than the ten righteous needed to save a place like Sodom. There are many here who care for this city.

Think about your church and the greater church in your city. Are there at least ten honorable people who sincerely care about your community? The Lord said He would spare Sodom for the sake of the ten.

JUST ONE

Abraham stopped praying at ten. But I will tell you something that is most profound: *Abraham stopped too soon.* The Lord reveals that His mercy will extend even further. Listen to what He told Jeremiah:

> Roam to and fro through the streets of Jerusalem, and look now, and take note. And seek in her open squares, if you can find a man, if there is one who does justice, who seeks truth, then I will pardon her.   —Jer 5:1

He says, "if you can find a man . . . then I will pardon her." One holy person in an evil city can actually turn away God's wrath. One godly individual who cares for a city (or a family or a school or a neighborhood or a church) swings open the door for mercy.

If just one soul refuses to give in to the intimidation of increasing wickedness, if that one refuses to submit to hopelessness, fear or unbelief, it is enough to exact from heaven a delay on wrath. *You*, my friend, can be that one who obtains forgiveness for your city until revival comes!

Mercy far outweighs wrath. You see, whenever a person operates in intercessory mercy, the tender passions of Christ are unveiled in the world. Do you want to truly know who Jesus is? Consider: He ever lives to make intercession; He is seated at the right hand of God the Father praying on our behalf (Heb 7:25; Rom 8:34). He is not eagerly waiting in heaven desiring an opportunity to destroy the world. He is praying for mercy. This is His nature.

Christ, the second person of the Trinity, is God in His mercy form. He is God loving the world, dying for its sins, paying the price of redemption. Christ is the mercy of God satisfying the justice of God.

When God declared that man was to be made in the divine image, it is this image of Christ the Redeemer that reveals our pattern. We are to follow the mercy path set by Christ. The Bible says to us, "as He is, so also are we in this world" (1 John 4:17).

Thus, the nature of Christ is manifest in our world every time redemptive intercession is offered to God on behalf of sinners. Jesus came to earth to fulfill the mercy of God. His title is Redeemer. His role is Savior. He is the Good Shepherd who lays down His life for His sheep. God calls us to be like Jesus, who says to us, "as the Father has sent Me, I also send you" (John 20:21). We are sent by Jesus with the purpose of Jesus: redemption.

The manifestation on earth of one Christlike intercessor perfectly restrains God's need for judgment on a society. Let me say it again: "Mercy triumphs over judgment" (James 2:13). Mercy plays exactly into God's heart. And one man or woman who reveals Christ's heart on earth will defer God's judgment from heaven.

Lord Jesus, forgive me for devaluing the power of prayer. Forgive me for underestimating how passionately You desire to reveal Your mercy. Lord, give me grace to be one who never ceases to cry out to You for mercy. Lord, let me not base my obedience on what my eyes see or my ears hear but, upon the revelation of Your mercy, let me build my life to Thee. AMEN!

CHAPTER FIVE

PRAYER CHANGES THE MIND OF GOD

LIFE OF THE INTERCESSOR

In the last chapter we gazed at the effect of mercy on the heart of God: the Lord would spare Sodom for the sake of ten righteous souls. We also discovered that God's mercy would have gone ever further. Even as the Lord's wrath was about to fall on Jerusalem, the Lord said if there had been just one man of integrity in the city, the man's presence could have gained pardon for the entire city (Jer 5:1).

Yet, the Lord's willingness to extend mercy has not always been welcomed by the church. We must rediscover true, basic Christianity. We have been content to possess a religion about what Jesus did without actually manifesting the reality of who Jesus is. Truly, our destiny does not find sure footing until the life of Christ emerges through us.

This Christlike transformation of the church was of the utmost concern for Paul. "My children," he wrote, "with whom I am again in labor until Christ is formed in you" (Gal 4:19). Christianity is nothing less than Christ Himself entering our lives and taking our form.

Again, Paul wrote, this time to the Corinthians: "For we who live are constantly being delivered over to death for Jesus' sake, that the life of Jesus also may be manifested in our mortal flesh" (2 Cor 4:11).

Do we see this? This is basic Christianity: the "life of Jesus . . . manifested in our mortal flesh." Anything less than Jesus' very life revealed through us will never satisfy our thirst to know the substance of God.

When we accepted Christ into our lives, it was not only that we would gain passage to heaven, but that He could again find passage to earth. Our salvation gives Jesus flesh and blood access for bringing mercy toward the specific needs of our world.

Paul said he was in spiritual travail, "labor," to see the life of Christ formed in the church. What is the life of Christ? To the church in Philippi he explained it this way:

Have this attitude in yourselves which was also in Christ Jesus, who, although He existed in the form of God, did not regard equality with God a thing to be grasped, but emptied Himself, taking the form of a bond-servant, and being made in the likeness of men. And being found in appearance as a man, He humbled Himself by becoming obedient to the point of death, even death on a cross.   –Phil 2:5–8

Christ is the Redeemer of the world; its Savior. Such characteristics are unfamiliar to us. However, it means we seek for mercy to triumph, for redemption to succeed, and God to be glorified in all things. To attain Christ's mind, God calls us to a realignment of our thoughts, attitudes, and motives until we think and act in perfect synchrony with Christ's nature.

We will not arrive at this overnight; it is a lifetime pursuit. Yet it means we set our goal not to be judgmental, but redemptive in our motives. We shun personal ambition and self-righteousness, replacing them with humility and love-motivated courage.

Think of it: We have been granted access to, or possession of, the very mind of Christ! This is not a doctrinally based mind, but a mercy-based view of life. An entirely new paradigm born of Christ's redemptive motive is destined to arise in those who seek Christlikeness.

Consider: From His vantage point of "equality with God" in eternity, Christ saw the world in all its sinfulness. He beheld the very worst of man's blood lust and immorality. The Lord beheld the long Dark Ages that blanketed Christianity. He contemplated the carnage of hundreds of wars throughout time, and specifically the two great wars that stormed through our world this past century. He knew there would be abortions, ethnic cleansing, witchcraft and human sacrifices. He was conscious of the fact that the entertainment industry would exploit man's fallen nature and that there would be those who would dedicate themselves to promoting sexual lust and violence throughout the world.

Having seen the sin that the world would commit, amazingly He did not condemn the world. Instead, He died for it. It is in this regard that Paul urges us, "Have this mind in you which was also in Christ Jesus" (Phil 2:5 KJV). This is the new paradigm: Our perception of the world must conform to what perfect love would do in all things.

How do we know if we have possessed the mind of Christ? Any time mercy-based, intercessory prayer manifests through us, the "mind . . . which was also in Christ Jesus" is functioning in us. Indeed, whenever Christ has a human counterpart praying on earth, Christ's prayer *through His intercessor* becomes the prevailing influence in the Godhead.

INTERCESSION: THE ESSENCE OF CHRIST

Throughout all ages Christ has revealed Himself through the intercession of the saints; the mercy prayer triumphs, whether our examples lived in Old or New Testament times. Was judgment for sin imminent? When Christ was revealed through redemptive intercession, divine wrath was restrained, delayed or even averted. Had Israel become wanton? When mercy pleads for time, though iniquity still abounds, grace abounds even more.

Since the advent of the New Testament, God has purposed to raise up an army of Christ-filled individuals whose prayers and actions multiplied mercy opportunities for God. Yet there have *always* been intercessors and visionaries whose prayers turned the heart of God from judgment to mercy. One such individual was Moses.

Moses exemplifies a man growing through the stages of intercession. Although he was born an Israelite, as an infant he was taken by Pharaoh's daughter and raised as an Egyptian.

During his first forty years, Moses was "educated in all the learning of the Egyptians" and became a man "of power in words and deeds" (Acts 7:22).

As he matured, however, a time came when he could no longer remain detached from the sufferings of his Israelite brethren; he began to identify with the people of God. Here is how the book of Hebrews renders this transition in Moses' life:

> By faith Moses, when he had grown up, refused to be called the son of Pharaoh's daughter; choosing rather to endure ill-treatment with the people of God, than to enjoy the passing pleasures of sin. —Heb 11:24–25

The Scriptures explain that when we number ourselves with others in need we are actually, in some fashion, revealing the nature of Christ (see Isa 53). Hebrews 11:26 confirms this, saying that when Moses chose to endure ill-treatment with the people of God, he was, in fact, bearing "the reproach of Christ."

Christ is God; He is the fulness of the Godhead in bodily form and thus, beyond reproach. However, the reproach Christ bears comes from His identification with sinners. The Pharisees reproached Christ because He accepted the ungodly into His company. Moses united himself with the humiliation and dehumanization of his brethren, who were slaves in Egypt. Yet, in so doing, he discovered that the reproach of Christ was "greater riches than the treasures of Egypt" (Heb 11:26).

The quickening in Moses was actually a Christ awakening. However, though Moses was awakened spiritually, he had not yet been trained. He was still immature and unfamiliar with the ways of God. His heart was open to Christ, but his mind was still in control of his decisions; in presumption he murdered an Egyptian. The Lord will not reject us for our fleshly beginnings, but neither will He endorse them. They invariably fail to bring deliverance.

Moses fled and spent forty years in the wilderness. There, alone with God, his pride and self-will were broken. Indeed, without brokenness no man can serve the Lord. Brokenness is openness to God. When the Lord finally sent Moses back, he went with true power as the leader of Israel and its intercessor.

What is a spiritual leader? He is one who is given the task of bringing God's promise to an imperfect people, and then he remains committed in prayer for that people until God's promise comes to pass. This is the nature of true intercession. Though we may indeed hate the sin that holds people in bondage, we cannot despise people for their rebellion and unbelief; this is the very reason they need our prayer!

Throughout Israel's long wilderness journey, Moses positions himself between the imminent judgment of God and God's mercy. Over and over again, he secures forgiveness from the Almighty which allows the people of Israel, even in their imperfections, to move forward. Throughout the entire journey Moses stays before God, never abandoning his role as intercessor; never doubting God's willingness to forgive the people. Remember, his task is to bring an imperfect people from "promise to fulfillment."

Moses himself was not perfect or immune to his own fleshly reactions. Frequently, he had to deal with Israel's criticism of himself and Aaron. Often, the Israelites fell into unbelief, murmuring and complaining against him, and he grew angry. Yet, he never failed to deal with his attitude and return to prayer for Israel.

At the same time, Moses himself was learning God's ways. An important lesson came when Amalek rose up to war against Israel. Moses said to Joshua,

"Choose men for us, and go out, fight against Amalek. Tomorrow I will station myself on the top of the hill with the staff of God in my hand." And Joshua did as Moses told him, and fought against Amalek; and Moses, Aaron, and Hur went up to the top of hill.

So it came about when Moses held his hand up, that Israel prevailed, and when he let his hand down, Amalek prevailed. But Moses' hands were heavy. Then they took a stone and put it under him, and he sat on it; and Aaron and Hur supported his hands, one on one side and one on the other. Thus his hands were steady until the sun set. So Joshua overwhelmed Amalek and his people with the edge of the sword.

—Ex 17:9–13

Moses realized that Israel's victory was attached to his posture before God. As leaders and intercessors, the victory that God's people are reaching for is often, in some measure, attached to our stand before God. The position of leaders in the "prayer posture" will add victory to the people in the "fight posture."

There are marriages in your neighborhood that are going to have a breakthrough because you stand before God with your hands lifted in prayer. There are breakthroughs in schools that will come, not because anyone is doing anything differently, but because you have placed yourself before God and are in prayer. Police will arrest criminals quicker because the church lifts its hands in prayer.

The person who stands before God and prays is valuable to God and instrumental in gaining the victory. Years ago I pastored a small church in Iowa. Almost without fail, each night I would pray for the congregation before I went to sleep. One night, however, I forgot to pray. Seven-thirty the next morning I received a call: One of the men in the church had been in a serious accident. Immediately I thought, "I did not pray last night," but then I dismissed it. I did not want to accept that my lack of prayer could have in any way contributed to what happened.

About six months later, again I went to sleep without praying for the church. And again, the next morning I woke to a distressing phone call. One of the farmers in the church had been harvesting when both his feet were caught and mangled in a jammed auger. Again, I thought, "I didn't pray last night," but once more I did not want to accept that people's lives could be left vulnerable by my lack of prayer. Still, the fear of God was on me because of these two accidents, so I made sure of my effort to intercede for my congregation nightly.

The following summer I spoke at a Christian camp and brought my family with me. My youngest son asked me to lie down with him that night. Exhausted, I laid down next to him and instantly we both fell asleep. When I came home from the camp I had another phone call waiting: A young woman in the church had rolled her car and crashed into a ditch. I knew the Lord was revealing to me something that I could no longer resist accepting: *my lack of prayer left people vulnerable to the enemy.*

Although all three of these people recovered from their injuries, I have never recovered from not praying at night. I often find myself waking in the middle of the night, interceding for various individuals or situations. As a leader or intercessor, God gives us spiritual authority to protect those whom we love. As wide as our range of love, to that degree we have authority in prayer. Such is the unique place we have, whether we are praying for our family, our church, city or nation, people will receive certain victories and protection that they otherwise would not have.

Let me share another example about the power of intercession to protect people. Several years ago, for a period of two weeks, pastors gathered each weekday at noon for prayer; we were specifically praying for our city and our local mayor. During this time our mayor and his wife came to Christ and each made a radical commitment to serve Him. However, within the next four months the enemy challenged the direction God was taking the city, and our community experienced three murders. The mayor and a couple of pastors consulted together and it was decided to meet in his office for prayer on Wednesday mornings at six. This prayer continued until his term was up (he chose to not run again). But throughout that time and for a year and a half afterwards, there was not another murder in the city—a total of more than thirty months!

When leaders and intercessors pray, God protects.

DON'T LEAVE GOD ALONE!

As we return to our study of Moses, again we see that Israel has sinned, this time constructing a golden calf, an idol, made from their melted jewelry. The Lord spoke to

Moses, "Go down at once, for your people, whom you brought up from the land of Egypt, have corrupted them- selves" (Ex 32:7). Remember, the glory of God has descended over the whole of Mount Sinai, three million Israelites are encamped at the foot of this mountain and a pillar of fire has settled in blazing glory on the mountain peak. Into this glory, Moses climbed and remained for forty days (Ex 24:18). At first Israel was terrified. Then, when Moses delayed his return, the people made a golden calf to worship as an idol. They lived in full view of the glory of God and then defied God's glory with their idolatry.

The Lord said to Moses, "I have seen this people, and behold, they are an obstinate people. Now then let Me alone, that My anger may burn against them, and that I may destroy them; and I will make of you a great nation" (Ex 32:9–10).

This is an amazing verse. The Lord says, "Let Me alone." As long as Moses *does not* let God alone, the Lord will not destroy Israel. *This is the only time our direct disobedience brings pleasure to the Lord.* Moses refuses to leave the ear and heart of God. Why? Because if there is one man standing in the gap, God's mercy stays kindled.

The goal of an intercessor is to not let God alone. The goal of the devil is to separate you from standing before God for your family, your city, your church, or your school. If the Lord has no intercessor, potentially His wrath may be kindled. "Let Me alone," the Lord says, yet Moses refuses. He is compelled by God's very mercy to disobey.

Moses has become a mature intercessor: He stays close to God, prevailing in prayer. Even though the Lord says He will make of Moses a great nation, Moses ignores the prospect. He knows that no matter what people he must lead, there will be problems, sin, and failure. No, Moses has come too far to start over. And then he reminds the Lord of the promise He made to Abraham, Isaac, and Jacob. This journey is about a covenant that was made with Israel's forefathers.

Remember, the assignment is to bring an imperfect people with a promise from God into fulfillment. The intercessor's role is to pray from the beginning of that journey, through the valleys of sin and setbacks, and continue praying until the promise from God is obtained.

You may be a pastor of a church or an intercessor or a parent. However, whatever you are praying for, you must have the attitude: *Lord, I am not letting You alone concerning this people.* Never pray for judgment or wrath; always pray for mercy. Such is the heart that brings heaven to earth and fulfillment to promises.

So the Lord changed His mind about the harm which He said He would do to His people.

—Ex 32:14

May this be a revelation to us all! *Moses' prayer changed God's mind!*

You may have a rebellious child or a mean-spirited boss or someone in your neighborhood who is pushing everyone to the limit. Instinctively, we desire that God would punish the individual who has wronged us. It is here that we must refuse to take our battles personally. Publicly, Moses was very upset with Israel; privately he pleaded with God for mercy, and he changed God's mind.

This is another reason why Jesus said we will not know the day or the hour when the time of great judgment would begin, because prayer can change the mind of God. In fact, Jesus tells us to "pray that your flight may not be in the winter" (Matt 24:20). We minimize it, but prayer actually can influence the season when the Great Tribulation begins.

Much of how God relates to a nation, city, church, or group is based upon how the people in that society pray. Prayer or lack of prayer sits at the table in the counsel of God's will. For Moses and the Israelites the outcome was profound: "So the Lord changed His mind about the harm which He said He would do to His people." Think of it: prayer changed God's mind.

Lord, thank You for always remaining entreatable to our cry. Help me to persevere, to give You no rest, until You fulfill Your highest purposes with this nation. Thank You that one voice is not too feeble that You cannot hear it, but that You will respond even to one intercessor who stands with You for the cause of mercy.

CHAPTER SIX

PARDON FOR AN UNREPENTANT PEOPLE

"ACCORDING TO YOUR WORD"

M oses sent twelve spies to Canaan to bring back a report of the land. When they returned, ten said that, though the land was good, Israel would surely be defeated by the inhabitants. Although Joshua and Caleb argued that Israel certainly could drive out their enemies, the people moaned, complained, and rebelled, even seeking to stone Joshua and Caleb and return with new leaders to Egypt. And again, the anger of the Lord was kindled against them and threatened to bring judgment (see Num 12–14).

Faithfully, once more Moses intercedes.

"I pray, let the power of the Lord be great, just as Thou hast declared. The Lord is slow to anger and abundant in lovingkindness, forgiving iniquity and transgression; but He will by no means clear the guilty, visiting the iniquity of the fathers on the children to the third and the fourth generations." —Num 14:17–18

Just as Abraham had prayed centuries before him, Moses focuses upon two things: the integrity of the Lord and His great mercy. God is slow to anger, He is abundant in lovingkindness, He forgives people. When the Scripture says He will "by no means clear the guilty," it speaks of those who sin yet do not repent. Yet even here the Lord is able to be entreated.

Remember, the Israelites have rebelled, they are not even aware that their sin has them at the threshold of God's wrath. The Lord looks at a nation of unrepentant, sinful people on one side and one man, Moses, praying on the other. Even though Moses acknowledges that the Lord will not "clear the guilty," Moses still prays that God would forgive Israel,

> "Pardon, I pray, the iniquity of this people according to the greatness of Thy lovingkindness, just as Thou also hast forgiven this people, from Egypt even until now."   —Num 14:19

Listen in awe at the Lord's response to Moses' mercy prayer. He says, "I have pardoned them according to your word" (Num 14:20).

Incredible!

Three million Israelites had not repented, nor rent their hearts, nor confessed their sins to God and one another. Not one of them who sinned possessed a broken, contrite spirit. Yet, the Lord says, "I have pardoned them." This is utterly amazing to me. The Lord granted Israel forgiveness "according to [Moses'] word."

Staggering!

One man with favor from God brought mercy upon three million people who had not repented.

Then, in case we think this is some kind of easy grace, the Lord reaffirms His purpose with all nations, beginning with Israel. He says, "But indeed, as I live, all the earth will be filled with the glory of the Lord" (Num 14:21).

The integrity of the Lord is non-negotiable. He says, in effect, *Though I forgive, I am not going to change My plans. All the earth will be filled with My glory.*

When we ask God for mercy, we are not asking Him to compromise His intentions. We are only asking that He forgive the sins of people until He can fulfill His purpose. In truth, we are in complete agreement with His desire. We earnestly want His glory to overshadow America, to fall upon Canada, to roll through Europe and Asia, Israel and the Middle East—all over the world, in fact. We shout a resounding "Yes!" to the purpose of God. Fill America with Your glory, Lord. Fill Canada. Fill Europe. Fill Israel and Africa, Asia and Australia with Your majestic glory. But we also pray, until Your purposes are perfected, reveal Your mercy and forgive the sins of Your people.

We need a vision of God's ultimate destiny for our nation: America "will be filled with the glory of the Lord." He will hear our prayer for mercy as we reach, with Him, toward His ultimate goal. Do you doubt this? *The mercy prayer worked for Moses.* God brought Israel from Egypt to Canaan through the prayer of His servant.

You say, "But that was Moses, I am a nobody." Jesus said, "He who is least in the kingdom of heaven is greater" than the greatest prophets in the Old Testament (see Matt 11:11). How can that be? We have the power of Christ's blood covenant to aid our quest for mercy!

Yet, God indeed used Moses to bring an imperfect people from promise to fulfillment. Whether we are praying for our nation, our cities, our churches, or our family, the Lord will "pardon them according to your word."

AN INTERCESSOR IS COMMITTED

Then Moses returned to the Lord, and said, "Alas, this people has committed a great sin, and they have made a god of gold for themselves. But now, if Thou wilt, forgive their sin—and if not, please blot me out from Thy book which Thou hast written!"   —Ex 32:31–32

An intercessor gives up all personal advantage for the sake of those he prays for. Moses knows he has favor with God. Yet, he presents himself as a remarkable portrait of one irreversibly committed to Israel's transformation. He says, "If thou wilt, forgive their sin—and if not, please blot me out from Thy book."

Moses is saying, in effect, that he is not serving for individual gain or glory. The Lord's servant cannot be separated, blessed, honored, or pleased apart from the fulfillment of God's promise to Israel. If God will not forgive them, He cannot have Moses either. Israel and Moses have become a package deal.

Some have struggled with situations in their personal lives where they cannot seem to break through. Perhaps you are spending too much time on *your* needs and not enough time praying for others. Make a prayer list of people with desperate needs, and as you intercede for them, see if the Holy Spirit doesn't break through for you. Remember the story of Job. When he prayed for his friends, God healed him. *Intercession not only transforms the world, it transforms us.*

ONE MORE THOUGHT

Moses accomplished what the Lord gave him to do: Through him, God brought the Israelites from Egypt to the Promised Land.

The book of Psalms records the tremendous role Moses played in bringing Israel from Egypt to the Promised Land:

> They made a calf in Horeb, and worshiped a molten image. Thus they exchanged their glory for the image of an ox that eats grass. They forgot God their Savior, who had done great things in Egypt, wonders in the land of Ham, and awesome things by the Red Sea. Therefore He said that He would destroy them, had not Moses His chosen one stood in the breach before Him, to turn away His wrath from destroying them.
>
> —Ps 106:19–23

One man changed the mind of God.

But something happened on that journey that was not good for Moses. Israel was thirsty. This time, instead of striking the rock to bring water, the Lord told Moses to speak to it. Angered at the people for their sin, Moses struck the rock instead. This action disqualified Moses from entering the Promised Land (see Num 20:8–13).

I have often pondered this situation. It has grieved me that Moses went so far, yet could not enter. Then it occurred to me, *it is possible Moses couldn't enter the promises because there was no one praying for him in the hour of his sin.*

Everyone needs someone who will pray for them. You need to pray for your pastor, and pray for those who pray for others. Everyone has at least one place in their heart that is not yet transformed, an area that needs the intercession of Christ to emerge through a friend on their behalf. Even Moses, intercessor for millions, needed an intercessor to pray and stand in the breach of obedience in his own life.

Lord Jesus, I am awed at Your willingness to show mercy. You actually changed Your mind about judgment on sinners because of one man, Moses. Lord, in my world and times, let me be that one who so delights You, who is so intimate with You, that my prayer for mercy outweighs Your need to destroy the unsaved. May the favor You have given to me be multiplied to those who yet do not know You, and may it spread until all the earth is filled with Your glory!

CHAPTER SEVEN

GOD
TALKING TO GOD

We have been studying the influence that one mercy-motivated intercessor can have upon the heart of God. In this, we looked at Abraham and then expanded our study to Moses. The Lord heard the intercession of Moses as he stood between divine judgment and Israel's sin, and he stayed in the place of intercession until God's Word concerning Israel came to pass.

The cycle of Israel's sin and God's justice repeated itself time and again. In essence, it was always the same: Israel rebelled; God threatened destruction; Moses interceded; God forgave.

Yet, even as we are awed by the power and privilege of prayer, in the subconscious realms of our souls, for some, another thought forms. At first, it appears as a question; because it is left unattended, it mutates into a multi-tentacled doubt. As we watch the cycle of sin and intercession repeat, some wonder: *Why does Moses' attitude toward Israel seem so much more merciful than God's?*

The very idea seems blasphemous; we are instantly ashamed that we thought it. We bury it, but it stays alive within us. For it *does* appear that the Lord would have been harsh, destroying men, women and children, had Moses not entreated Him.

Of course, as good Christians, we dare not voice this doubt; we do not even whisper it to our most trusted friends. As a result, what ought to be a wonderful example of the value and power of prayer, instead, on a more basic level, causes us to mistrust God's goodness whenever our goodness fails.

Even if you are not personally struggling with this battle, someone you love probably is or will be. When people fall away from God, often it is because they doubt the goodness of God to forgive them. Thus, we need to clear this mystery concerning God's wrath and its relationship to man's prayer.

THE PURPOSE OF GOD

There is a revelation awaiting us about the nature of God—indeed, the nature of life itself—that will not only settle our doubts but will accelerate our pursuit of Christlikeness. The key that unlocks the mystery of divine judgment, and its power to compel us toward mercy, begins in the first chapter of Genesis. There, we discover that God has encoded into humanity a grand and irreversible purpose: We have been created to reveal the image and likeness of God.

Though the world scene has continually changed, the Lord has never changed nor deviated from this plan. Let's read as God Himself declared His purpose in the sacred Scriptures. The Lord said,

"Let Us make man in Our image, according to Our likeness . . . And God created man in His own image, in the image of God He created him; male and female He created them."

—Gen 1:26–27

Though we read that man was created in the divine image, let me suggest to you that, in Genesis, we are seeing a beginning, not a fulfillment. God's plan was only *initiated* in Eden. Although Adam and Eve possessed intelligence and freedom of will above that of the animals, the divine nature was far from full bloom.

You say, "Wait, the Bible said that God creat*ed* man in His own image. It is past tense." Yes. However, the faith-voice of the Holy Spirit often speaks of things to come as though they were already here. The Lord said to Abraham, "A father of many nations have I made you" (past tense). Yet, when we look at Abraham and Sarah, we see they were actually childless when they received God's promise (see Rom 4:17). In fact, when Sarah died, they had produced but one child, not many nations. As time progressed, many nations have, indeed, emerged from Abraham. God's Word is a historic, completed fact in eternity, but in the realm of time it is a truth yet to be manifest.

For further proof that Adam and Eve were not walking in the completed likeness of God, consider: Shortly after they were created, they fell into sin. If mankind were *functionally* created in the image and likeness of God, how is it that they sin? Can God sin? Sin is the one thing God *cannot* do.

So man's creation in the garden of Eden is really the commencement to a journey that would actually span the ages of time; man's history with God represents unfolding stages in that journey.

As we study the Bible, we learn that the Lord was serious about sin, both in Eden and also in Noah's day. Then, through Abraham, we discover that God exalts faith above works; to *believe* God is a form of righteousness that exceeds ritual obedience. In Moses' era, through the Law, God provided structure to concepts of righteousness and means to atone for man's failings. Finally, in Jesus Christ, God sums up all that He requires of man. He satisfies the demands of wrath and Law, and celebrates the triumph of mercy and grace. We behold the image and likeness of God in human form, and more: We see the true pattern to which God seeks to conform us.

The introduction of Christ into the consciousness of mankind is chronicled by the New Testament writers. Romans 8:28–30 reveals that Christ is the first-born of many predestined brethren. Galatians 2:20 and 2 Corinthians 13 explain that Christ is living in us now; while 2 Corinthians 3:18 assures us that, from the moment Christ entered our spirits, we began a process of transformation, where the Spirit conforms us, from glory to glory, into His image.

Finally, the full metamorphoses, from fallen sinner to man recreated in God's nature, will be accomplished at the end of the last trump of this dispensation. Our mortality will put on immortality and our corruptible will put on incorruption, and shall be like Him (1 Cor 15:53; 1 John 3:2). At that moment, all heaven will celebrate in awe and praise, "the mystery of God is finished" (Rev 10:7).

Adam never was the prototype. From eternity God's purpose was that man would be conformed to Jesus Christ. Paul tells us that God chose us in Christ *prior* to Adam's fall. Indeed, He chose us "before the foundation of the world" (Eph 1:4).

Thus, Adam's sin did not surprise the Lord. There was no moment of panic in heaven nor new adjustments to be made from the original plan. The fall of Adam and Eve was an event that unfolded on schedule. In other words, in His omniscience, the Lord knew man would sin, He calculated its effect, and incorporated man's fall into His plan before Adam even sinned.

This, however, is not to say that we are free to blame God for our failures. The Lord did not tempt Adam and Eve, nor did He in any way *cause* them to sin. Adam was specifically warned to avoid the tree of the knowledge of good and evil. The man knew there were consequences. God did not create man to experience sin, but to know genuine freedom. The Lord knew, however, that with freedom would come sin and that mankind's fall was inevitable.

As further evidence that man's sin was no surprise to God, consider well this thought: Christ is revealed in Scripture as the "Lamb slain from the foundation of the world" (Rev 13:8 NKJ; see also 1 Pet 1:18–20). Amazingly, *before* man sinned, his debt was paid. The fall allowed for a deepening of man's dependency upon God; it was an unavoidable component in divine purpose.

MAN & GOD TOGETHER IN REDEMPTION

There is something else in the Genesis account to consider. The Scriptures nearly always speak of the Almighty in *singular* terms. We read that God *(singular)* created the physical world. But then, when we read of man, the Almighty speaks in *plural* terms, saying, "Let *Us* make man . . ."

Theologically speaking, we define the Lord's ability to separate Himself from Himself without diminishing the essential oneness of His nature as the Trinity. The most visible example, of course, is the relationship between the Father and Son. Each time Jesus prayed to the Father, it was, in truth, God on earth talking with God in heaven: God separated from Himself, yet remained one with Himself.

Christ, as God's Son, is said to have been "begotten" by the Father. He is the same substance as God, yet separated organically from the Godhead by human flesh and subjective human experience. Yet, never was Christ separated from His oneness with the Father. As Christians, we accept the mystery of the Trinity even if we cannot fully understand it. However, this discovery of God's "separated oneness" leads us back to our original question: Is Moses more merciful than God?

Let us ask another question: *Who is the source and inspiration of Moses' prayer life?* The answer to this question will settle the mystery concerning prayer, mercy and the judgment of God. Let's look at what happened to Moses to bring him into his relationship with the Almighty.

We can imagine that the highly cultured Egyptians were shocked that Moses, now a mature and popular prince in Egypt, had become increasingly more concerned for the Hebrew slaves. After all, Moses was enjoying the finest conditions that civilization and position in life provided. There was nothing to gain, no personal advantage to be found, by identifying with Egypt's slaves. The Egyptians deemed the Israelites hardly more valuable than cattle. The idea of somehow helping the Hebrews was preposterous. Help them? As a prince in Egypt, Moses *owned* them!

Yet, Moses could not defend himself against the deepening burdens of his own heart. Even against his will, empathy toward the Hebrews was growing within him. From the moment he began to identify with the weaknesses, the injustices and the sufferings of his oppressed brethren, the Spirit of Christ began awakening him to his destiny. As we said earlier, this act of compassionate identification with those who are scorned, disgraced or discredited is called the *reproach of Christ,* which Moses considered to be "greater riches than the treasures of Egypt" (Heb 11:26).

Prior to this time, Moses was aloof and apathetic toward Israel's need. However, after Christ had worked in him, he had authority to deliver the Hebrews from slavery in Egypt and he had compassion to intercede for them in their sin. Thus we see that Moses was himself the product of Christ's mercy toward Israel.

The Lord revealed Himself perfectly in the New Testament; however, He also made Himself evident frequently *through people* in the Old Testament. Indeed, *whenever* we read of intercessory prayer or redemptive action on the part of one for the need of many, it is actually Christ manifesting through that individual. Moses bore *Christ's* reproach.

The question of whether Moses is more merciful than God proves to be superfluous, for the spirit of intercession emerging through Moses is not Moses, but Christ praying *through* him on behalf of man. Man is not more merciful than God; God is using man to manifest His mercy! What we actually are seeing operating through human instrumentality is God in His mercy interceding before God in His justice. *At the highest level, intercessory prayer is God talking to God through man.*

Remember, we said earlier that God separates Himself from Himself, yet never loses His essential oneness with Himself in the Godhead. When the Lord appears ready to reveal His wrath, He will always, simultaneously, be searching for an individual through whom Christ can emerge in the mercy prayer.

Without doubt God *must* reveal His righteous judgment concerning sin, otherwise mercy has no meaning or value. In the Godhead, the Father is revealed as God in authority and justice; Christ is God revealed in redemptive mercy; the Holy Spirit is God in manifest power. Yet, the goal of the Godhead is not only to display all the aspects of the divine nature, but to unveil the Almighty in His highest glory: love.

As Christians, our call is to manifest the voice and mercy of Christ to God. In intercessory prayer and mercy-motivated action, we identify with those exiled from heaven because of sin; and we unite with those separated from God because of heartache, physical suffering, or persecution. In manifesting the redemptive mercy of God, we embrace the very reason for our existence: to be transformed into Christ's image.

MORE PERFECT THAN PARADISE

God so designed life that a significant measure of the administration of mercy would only come through *human* agencies. He tells Moses,

"Behold, the cry of the sons of Israel has come to Me; furthermore, I have seen the oppression with which the Egyptians are oppressing them. Therefore, come now, and I will send you to Pharaoh." —Ex 3:9–10

The Lord says, "I have seen the oppression . . . I will send you." God sees the need, but He reveals His mercy through His servant. Whether we are speaking of Moses' intercession or the temple offerings of the Jewish priests or the most perfect act of intercession, Christ's incarnation and death, God's mercy finds its greatest manifestation through human instrumentality.

When we hear that the Spirit of God is threatening wrath, the very fact that He is warning us first gives us the opportunity, even with fear and trembling, to embrace the role of Christ-inspired intercession. He desires that we touch His heart with mercy, thus averting wrath. In truth, the primary reason God warns is not so we can run and hide, but so we can stand and pray. He seeks to inspire mercy in His people. Even when the Almighty shows Himself angered or grieved and poised for judgment, He tells us that He is still seeking a means of mercy. He says, "I searched for a man among them who should . . . stand in the gap before Me for the land, that I should not destroy it" (Ezek 22:30).

We can expect that the Lord would thrust us into times of desperation where we would face genuine calamities or fearful situations. He does this in order that we truly participate with Him in the redemptive purpose. And it is here, whether our cry is for our children or church, our city or country, that we are compelled toward God for mercy; in desperation, we grasp and attain the nature of Christ.

Adam's sin and subsequent expulsion from Eden seemed the worst of all possible events; yet, to the Almighty, there were lessons man needed to learn about mercy and love that could not be taught in Paradise. Indeed, what looks like an imperfect environment to us is actually the perfect place to create man in the likeness of God. Here, we have a realm suitable for producing tested virtue. In this fallen world, character can be proven genuine and worship made pure and truly precious. Yes, it is here where we truly discover the depths of God's love in sending Christ to die for our sin. And here, in the fire of life-and-death realities, where we become like Him.

Lord Jesus, Your love, Your sacrifice is the pattern for my life. How I desire to be like You. I want more than anything to reveal Your mercy, both to the world and also to the Father. I surrender all my other rights and privileges that I may possess this glorious gift of conformity to You. I love You, Lord. Use me, pray through me, love through me until, in all things, I reflect Your image and likeness.

CHAPTER EIGHT

THE BELOVED

We have been talking about prayer, Christlikeness, and the future of America. I would like to continue that focus, but look at the manifestation of Christ on earth as it impacts the Father. There is something utterly pleasing to the Father when Christ is revealed. It actually goes far beyond not destroying the wicked; it touches His heart in the depths of His nature.

Thus, to satisfy God, we must perceive what the Son presents to the Father in terms of their relationship. Let us, therefore, consider first the weightiness of having Jesus Christ as our mediator with God.

Jesus says that the Father has loved Him from "before the foundation of the world" (John 17:24). The love that exists between the Father and the Son transcends the boundaries of time. Before the ages began or the stars were young; before the earth, man or angels were created, the Father and Son have known only love. Their union within the Trinity is so complete that, though they are two distinct personalities, the Scripture can state with perfect fidelity: "The Lord our God is one God."

During His ministry, Jesus spoke frequently of this love between the Father and Himself. He said, "The Father loves the Son, and has given all things into His hand" (John 3:35). Again we read, "For the Father loves the Son, and shows Him all things that He Himself is doing" (John 5:20). And again, "I love the Father, and as the Father gave Me commandment, even so I do" (John 14:31).

In Jesus' first public appearance, this love between Father and Son engulfed the scene at the river Jordan. While Jesus was still in the water, "heaven was opened, and the Holy Spirit descended upon Him in bodily form like a dove, and a voice came out of heaven, 'Thou art My beloved Son, in Thee I am well-pleased' " (Luke 3:21–22).

Do not rush past this phrase, "My beloved Son." Jesus is not just "a son," or even "the Son," He is the Father's *"beloved* Son." There is no one like Him. Here, in this incredible, inaugural moment, the Father Himself draws near. Almighty God moves from His throne in the highest heaven until His face is at the edge of our physical world. From eternity the Father speaks to His Son: "In Thee I am well-pleased."

Then, the Almighty turns and repeats the identical thought to John the Baptist, the forerunner of Christ: "This is My beloved Son, in whom I am well-pleased" (Matt 3:17).

Note: in both times that He spoke, the Father could not help but express His love for Jesus. In truth, the Father is consumed with love for His Son.

We do not have a human reference to understand the energy, the passion, and the unrestrained oneness that exists between the Father and the Son. We can only stand and watch in awe, and learn of it. It is the essence of heaven; it is the nectar of eternal life.

"Beloved . . . in Thee I am well-pleased."

The deep, unfathomable perfection of God, the incomprehensible ethos of the divine nature, knows only pleasure in Jesus. The Almighty, who gives to all life, receives life from the Son and is fulfilled to the depth of His being. The Father gazes at His Son and harbors no slight shadow of regret, no lingering wish for someone or something to be done better. We behold God on earth satisfying God in heaven: perfect surrender in the embrace of perfect acceptance.

Their relationship is amazing. Yet, add to it the fact that, prior to this encounter, Jesus had not accomplished any miracles; there were no signs or wonders, no vast multitudes. Outwardly, a carpenter named Jesus came, like everyone else, to be baptized. Until that moment, Jesus' life was unremarkable. He was another woodworker.

How was it that, even in the common tasks of an ordinary life, Jesus drew the praise of heaven? At the core of His being, He only did those things which pleased the Father. In everything, He stayed true, heartbeat to heartbeat, with the Father's desires. Jesus lived for God alone; God was enough for Him. Thus, even in its simplicity and moment-to-moment faithfulness, Christ's life was an unending fragrance, a perfect offering of incomparable love to God.

Privately, the unfolding stream of divine passion from the Father for Jesus never abated; the Jordan was but the first public exchange. We see other references as we proceed through the Scriptures. Look at Matthew's account, chapter 12. Christ's public ministry has begun. Listen to how that which was written from eternity past again describes their holy relationship. Many are following and He is healing them all, yet He bids the multitudes to not make Him known.

> In order that what was spoken through Isaiah the prophet, might be fulfilled, saying, "Behold, My Servant whom I have chosen; My beloved in whom My soul is well-pleased; I will put My Spirit upon Him, and He shall proclaim justice to the Gentiles." —Matt 12:17–18

Listen to the sacred text, the prophetic word chosen to describe the Father and His beloved. God cannot speak of Christ, or even make reference to Him, without calling Him "My beloved in whom My soul is well-pleased."

One day, indeed, we will gaze upon the face of God's beloved and we will know that to see His face is the highest blessedness of heaven.

Again, look in Matthew 17. On the holy mountain Jesus was magnificently transfigured before three of His disciples. His face shone like the sun. His garments became white as light, flashing like lightning. Moses and Elijah appeared, talking with Christ. Into this splendor, Peter nervously presented an idea. While he was still speaking, a radiant cloud formed and then overshadowed the disciples. Out from this living splendor, again, the voice of God was heard:

> "This is My beloved Son, with whom I am well-pleased; listen to Him!" —Matt 17:5

The all-knowing, all-wise God, the Creator of heaven and earth, in the only times He has ever spoken audibly to mankind, has said the same thing three times: "This is My beloved Son." In all the unlimited creativity of the mind of God, there is nothing more profound, no greater revelation than to say, "Listen to Him!"

In each occasion that He speaks, the Father returns to glorifying His beloved. We hear this information, we write it down, we think we grasp God's truth; but we do not. We underline but do not understand. Too quickly we seek to move to another insight, but the voice of God brings us back. In the Father's eyes, there is no other truth. We have not genuinely understood who Jesus is, otherwise we would feel as the Father does.

This love within the Godhead is the symphony of the universe. It is what makes heaven heavenly. Even as we are awed by such all-consuming oneness, Jesus asks that each of us, as His disciples, would be included in this holy hymn of heaven. He prays, "O righteous Father . . . I have made Thy name known to them, and will make it known; that the love wherewith Thou didst love Me may be in them, and I in them" (John 17:25–26).

Jesus prays that the same love, the same overwhelming fulfillment that the Father has in His Son, may also be manifested in us. In other words, God desires that *we* become as totally consumed with Jesus as is the Father!

WHAT CHRIST PROVIDES

But this is a book about intercession for America. How, then, does the love between the Father and the Son connect us to America and praying for its need?

To answer that, let me pose this question: What is it, uniquely, that the Father has found in the Son that so fulfills Him? I believe the Son's gift is this: Jesus presents to the Father the opportunity to satisfy His deepest passions and to reveal His highest glory, the nature of which is love.

We see this in Jesus' statement, "For this reason the Father loves Me, because I lay down My life" (John 10:17). The Son presents to the Father reconciliation between heaven and earth. He allows God to be revealed as He truly is: not a harsh judge but a loving Father.

Perhaps it is incomprehensible to us that God could suffer or feel pain, yet Scriptures reveal that the Spirit of God relates in interactive union with this world. In His eternal nature, the Father sees man's end from the beginning. However, in His relationship with mankind's journey through time, the Scriptures are plain, the heart of God is vulnerable to humanity.

In Noah's day, we read that the Lord was "grieved in His heart" (see Gen 6:3–6). The Psalms revealed that Israel "grieved Him in the desert" (Ps 78:40). The word "grieved" meant to "worry, pain or anger." We know that, when a sinner repents, there is increased joy among angels (Luke 15:7), but what happens in heaven when God is grieved?

You see, the Lord participated vicariously in the suffering of His people. Indeed, in Judges we are told of a time when "He could bear the misery of Israel no longer" (Judges 10:16).

Consider: the Spirit of God was not aloof, separated from Israel's condition. Just as the Spirit hovered over the pre-creation world, so He brooded over Israel, being deeply involved, moved to the point of being unable to "bear the misery of Israel" any longer.

Since mankind's fall, there has been a restless longing in the heart of God toward man. Indeed, if we are unreconciled with someone whom we love, do we not also carry heartache until we are restored? By providing atonement for man's sins, Jesus heals the estrangement, the wound, in the Father's heart, and then He extends that healing to man.

Paul explains what Christ has done in his letter to the Colossians. He writes:

> And when you were dead in your transgressions and the uncircumcision of your flesh, He made you alive together with Him, having forgiven us all our transgressions, having canceled out the certificate of debt consisting of decrees against us and which was hostile to us; and He has taken it out of the way, having nailed it to the cross.
>
> —Col 2:13–14

Mankind's unpayable debt is paid; God's incurable wound, healed. Not only do we have peace with God through the sacrifice of Christ, God has peace with us. He is freed from the limitations of justice; now He can remove the penalty of sin through love.

Let us celebrate what Christ has done: The demands of divine wrath, which could not be settled by man, are fully settled by God Himself through Christ. God is longing for reconciliation and healing with humanity. Indeed, Jesus said, "The kingdom of heaven may be compared to a certain king who wished to settle accounts" (Matt 18:23). This is God's heart, through Christ: He desires to *settle accounts with mankind!*

As long as we ourselves abide in mercy, the full panorama of divine mercy will remain open and fully active toward mankind's need. When we pray, "in Jesus' name," we are coming to the Father with the goal of mercy in mind. The announcement that we have come "in Jesus' name" signifies we are representatives of Jesus' purpose, which is mercy and not judgment.

COME BOLDLY FOR MERCY!

The Father has never taken pleasure in the death of the wicked. The idea that He has enjoyed destroying sinners is a satanic slander which Christ came to dispel. His attitude toward mankind is exactly the opposite: His joy increases when sinners repent. Because Christ's sacrifice for sin has led to millions who have repented, Jesus has increased inestimably the Father's joy.

Because judgment is now atoned for in Christ, the Father has full freedom to answer every prayer of mercy. He no longer is constrained to decide between judgment and mercy; mercy triumphs over judgment!

The church can come boldly into the throne of God's grace and stand before the mercy seat in prayer for the world around us. This is what Jesus gives to the Father: perfect fulfillment of God's love, perfect fulfillment of His compassion, perfect unveiling of the highest glory of God.

In fact, the very inspiration to intercede is the result of Christ working within us. Every time Christ is revealed through our intercession, wrath is delayed and divine mercy begins searching for the opportunity to triumph. When we pray, "God be merciful," we are not merely delaying His wrath; in truth, we are delighting and fulfilling His heart for mercy!

Do you not also feel, increasing in you, the Father's love for Jesus? He brings heaven to earth and bids us to join Him in the redemptive purpose. To cover sin, to not condemn but rather to intercede, is to reveal the nature of

Christ. Whenever Christ is revealed, mercy triumphs, and the Father is well-pleased.

Lord Jesus, I desire to join You in bringing pleasure to the Father. Forgive me for my shallowness and indifference. Help me to see in You the pattern of love that never ceased to bring pleasure to the Father. You are the fragrance that pleases God. Come forth in Your mercy, even through me, and make me a source of delight unto the Father. Thank You, Lord, for You are my beloved, too, and in You, I find the river of God's pleasure.

CHAPTER NINE

HE WILL SPRINKLE MANY NATIONS

THE GIFT OF WOUNDEDNESS

The world and all it contains was created for one purpose: to showcase the grandeur of God's Son. In Jesus, the nature of God is magnificently and perfectly revealed; He is the expressed image of God. Yet, to gaze upon Christ is to also see God's pattern for man. As we seek to be like Him, we discover that our need was created for His sufficiency. We also see that, once the redemptive nature of Christ begins to triumph in our lives, mercy begins to triumph in the world around us.

How will we recognize revival when it comes? Behold, here is the awakening we seek: men and women, young and old, all conformed to Jesus. When will revival begin? It starts the moment we say "yes" to becoming like Him; it spreads to others as Christ is revealed through us.

Yet, to embrace Christ's attitude toward mercy is only a first step in our spiritual growth. There are other levels of transformation which call us to deeper degrees of surrender. Indeed, just as Jesus learned obedience through the things He suffered, so also must we (Heb 5:8). And it is here, even while we stand in intercession or service to God, that He gives us the *gift* of woundedness.

"Gift?" you ask. Yes, to be wounded in the service of love, and to remain committed to mercy, is to gain access to power in the redemptive purpose. The steadfast prayer of the wounded intercessor has great influence upon the heart of God.

We cannot become Christlike without experiencing woundedness. You see, even after we come to Christ, we carry encoded within us preset limits concerning how far we will go for love, and how much we are willing to suffer for redemption. The wounding exposes those human boundaries and reveals what we lack of His nature.

The path narrows as we seek true transformation. Indeed, many Christians fall short of Christ's stature because they have been offended. They leave churches discouraged, vowing never again to serve or lead or contribute because, when they offered themselves, their gift was marred by unloving people. To be wounded in the administration of mercy can become a great offense to us, especially as we are waiting for, and even expect, a reward for our good efforts.

Yet, wounding is inevitable if we will follow Christ. Jesus was both "marred" and "wounded" (Isa 52:14; Zech 13:6), and we will be as well. How else shall love be perfected?

Beware: Life offers few choices in dealing with our wounds. We either become Christlike and forgive or we enter a spiritual time warp where we abide continually in the memory of our wounding. Like a systemic disease, it destroys every aspect of our reality. In truth, apart from God, the wounding that life inflicts is incurable; God has decreed, only Christ in us can survive.

Intercessors live on the frontier of change. We are positioned to stand between the need of man and the provision of God. Because we are the agents of redemption, Satan will *always* seek means to offend, discourage, silence or otherwise steal the strength of our prayer. The wounding we receive must be interpreted in light of God's promise to reverse the effects of evil and make them work for good. Since spiritual assaults are inevitable, we must discover how God uses our wounds as the means to greater power. This was exactly how Christ brought redemption to the world.

Jesus knew that maintaining love and forgiveness in the midst of suffering was the key that unlocked the power of redemption. Isaiah 53:11 tells us, "By His knowledge the Righteous One, My Servant, will justify the many, as He will bear their iniquities."

Jesus possessed *revelation knowledge* into the mystery of God. He knew that the secret to unleashing world-transforming power was found at the cross. The terrible offense of the cross became the place of redemption for the world. Yet, remember, Jesus calls us to a cross as well. Wounding is simply an altar upon which our sacrifice to God is prepared.

Listen again to Isaiah's prophetic description of Jesus' life. He says something that at first seems startling, but as we read we discover a most profound truth concerning the power of woundedness. He writes,

But the Lord was pleased to crush Him, putting
Him to grief; if He would render himself as a

guilt offering, He will see His offspring, He will prolong His days, and the good pleasure of the Lord will prosper in His hand.   —Isa 53:10

How did Jesus obtain the power of God's pleasure and have it prosper in His hands? During His times of crushing, woundedness and devastation, instead of retaliating, He rendered Himself "as a guilt offering."

The crushing is not a disaster; it is an opportunity. Yet, the greater benefit ascends beyond the effect mercy has upon the sinner; it's the effect our mercy has on *God*. We want to be instruments of God's good pleasure; it is redemption, not wrath, which must prosper in our hands.

So, when Christ encounters conflict, even though He is the Lion of Judah, He comes as the Lamb of God. Even when He is outwardly stern, He is always mindful that, encoded into His DNA, He is the guilt offering. Thus, Jesus not only asks the Father to forgive those who have wounded Him, He numbers Himself *with* the transgressors and intercedes *for* them (see Isa 53:12). He does this because the Father takes no pleasure in the death of the wicked, and it is the pleasure of God that Jesus seeks.

Is this not the wonder and mystery, yes, and the power of Christ's cross? In anguish and sorrow, wounded in heart and soul, still He offered Himself for His executioner's sins. Without visible evidence of success, as an apparent failure before man, He courageously held true to mercy. In the depth of terrible crushing, He let love attain its most glorious perfection as He uttered the immortal words: "Father, forgive them; for they do not know what they are doing" (Luke 23:34).

Christ could have escaped. He told Peter as the Romans came to arrest Him, "Do you think that I cannot appeal to My Father, and He will at once put at My disposal more than twelve legions of angels?" (Matt 26:53) In less than a heartbeat the skies would have been flooded with thousands of warring angels. Yes, Jesus could have escaped, but mankind would have perished. Christ chose to go to hell for us rather than return to heaven without us. Instead of condemning mankind, He rendered *Himself* as the guilt offering. He prays the mercy prayer, "Father, forgive them . . ."

Jesus said, "He who believes in Me, the works that I do shall he do also" (John 14:12). We assume He meant that we would work His miracles, but Jesus did not limit His definition of "works" to the miraculous. The works He did–the redemptive life, the mercy cry, the identification with sinners, rendering Himself a guilt offering—*all* the works He did, we shall "do also."

Thus, because He lives within us, we see that Isaiah 53 does not belong exclusively to Jesus; it also becomes the blueprint for Christ in us. Indeed, was this not part of His reward, that He would see His offspring? (Isa 53:10) True Christians are the progeny of Christ.

Listen to Paul's heart, "Now I rejoice in my sufferings for your sake, and in my flesh I do my share on behalf of His body (which is the church) in filling up that which is lacking in Christ's afflictions" (Col 1:24).

What does the apostle mean? Did not Christ fully pay mankind's debts once for all? Is he implying that *we* now take *Jesus'* place? No. We will never take Jesus' place. *It means that Jesus has come to take our place.* The Son of God manifests all the aspects of His redemptive, sacrificial life through us. Indeed, "As He is, so also are we in this world" (1 John 4:17).

Not only does Paul identify with Christ in his personal salvation, he is consumed with Christ's purpose. He wrote, "That I may know Him, and the power of His resurrection and the fellowship of His sufferings, being conformed to His death" (Phil 3:10).

What a wondrous reality: this *fellowship* of His sufferings. Here, in choosing to yoke our existence with Christ's purpose, we find true friendship with Jesus. This is intimacy with Christ. The sufferings of Christ are not the sorrows typically endured by mankind; they are the afflictions of love. They bring us closer to Jesus as, together, we bring pleasure to God.

Listen to one more thought. The power of Christ is enough to cleanse and turn nations to God. Isaiah 53 is preceded by a grand announcement which heralds the effects of Christ's victory. It reads:

> Behold, My servant will prosper, He will be high and lifted up, and greatly exalted.
>
> Just as many were astonished at you, My people, so His appearance was marred more than any man, and His form more than the sons of men.
>
> Thus He will sprinkle many nations, kings will shut their mouths on account of Him; for what had not been told them they will see, and what they had not heard they will understand.
>
> —Isa 52:13–15

What does it mean, that He will "sprinkle many nations"? Under the Old Covenant, priests would take the blood of a sacrificed animal and, with it, sprinkle the temple and its furnishings. By so doing they cleansed and made holy that which was otherwise common and unclean. In the New Testament, every believer serves as a priest before the throne of God (Rev 1:6). We come to sprinkle that which is unclean in our world with the blood of Christ. God promises that, as Christ is revealed through us, the sacrifice of God's Lamb will sprinkle many nations; kings will see and understand.

Our call is to follow the Lamb through our personal woundedness into the triumph of love and redemption. In the area of woundedness, we ask not for wrath, but mercy. Whatever the issue—slander, unfaithfulness, desertion, rejection, racism or abuse—we render ourselves to God. The greater the pain in releasing and forgiving the sins against you, the purer your love becomes. Remember, the prayer of the wounded intercessor holds great sway upon God's heart.

What we become in our individual conformity to Christ may be, in its own way, even more important to God than the revival for which we are praying. Listen, my friends: Just as mankind shall look upon Him whom they pierced, and Christ's wounds shall be with Him forever (Zech 12:10), so *our* wounds will be recognized for what they are: entry points through which Christ's "eternal weight of glory" emanate through us (2 Cor 4:17).

In speaking both of the sprinkling of the nations as well as the manifestation of the Redeemer's life, Isaiah presents a question. He asks, "Who has believed our message? And to whom has the arm of the Lord been revealed?" (Isa 53:1) I write as one who has believed the report. The Scriptures tell us that love "bears all things, believes all things, hopes all things, endures all things.

Love never fails" (1 Cor 13:7–8). Yes, when Christ is revealed through the church, the power of redemption will prevail for our land, and mercy will certainly triumph over judgment.

Lord Jesus, for You I live; to be like You, may I be willing to die. Let redemption exult through me! Let mercy triumph through me! Do not allow me to withdraw from the fire of conformity to You. Create me in Your holy image, let love prevail through me!

PART TWO:

AMERICA AWAKENED TO GOD'S HIGHEST PURPOSE

Nations will come to your light.
—Isa 60:3 —

I would have despaired
unless I had believed that I would see
the goodness of the Lord
In the land of the living.

—Ps 27:13 —

CHAPTER TEN

AMERICA'S
UNFINISHED TASK

*The awesome solemnity of the role of the USA in
the post-"cold war" world is only now beginning to
dawn on many.*   *–Patrick Johnstone[1]*

To perceive America's future, we must appreciate its
past. Without stepping into pride or blind national-
ism, we need to esteem how God has used the United
States, especially since the 1940s. Indeed, just as the Lord
commanded Israel to recall their blessings and honor Him
for their victories so, with humility, we should call to mind
God's mighty hand upon this nation.

Let us not forget how, during World War II, the
Almighty empowered the U.S. to defeat Nazism and
Japanese imperialism. Then, for the next forty-five years,
the Lord manifested His resolve to arrest the advance of
Soviet communism, ultimately using the spiritual, eco-

---

[1] *Operation World,* page 564

nomic and military strength of America to topple this stronghold of atheism.

For more than sixty years, God Himself has maximized the global influence of the U.S. Beneath the shelter of American benevolence, and economic and military strength, Christianity has spread exponentially to many nations. It was God's hand upon this nation which played a significant role in opening the world for the sake of the gospel.

You say, "God doesn't need America. He could have snapped His fingers and immediately these evil empires would have crumbled." That's true. God could have used plagues, meteors, angels or other nations; He could have opened the ground and swallowed Germany, Japan and Russia in a heartbeat. Psalms 115:3 tells us that our "God is in the heavens; He does whatever He pleases." The Almighty can do anything He pleases in any way He pleases. Therefore, since He obviously chose to use America to defeat these demonic strongholds, we must conclude America was His *first* choice and using America is what pleased Him most.

RECENT HISTORY

One of the most significant consequences of World War II was that the number of nations leading the world dropped from five: Great Britain, Germany, Japan, Soviet Union and the United States, to two: the Soviet Union and the United States.

The Soviet bloc of nations covered one-sixth of the earth's land mass. For nearly fifty years, these two remaining superpowers competed with each other to possess the future of the world. Each nation reinforced its ideological position by continually increasing their military strength; every event on the world stage was an opportunity to advance international propaganda.

Eye to eye and weapon for weapon, neither nation would flinch or allow itself room to publicly lose face. Nuclear war was the unthinkable option: a dread specter in the world's subconsciousness. The threats and counter-threats of nuclear conflagration were not without substance: the U.S. had dropped two atomic bombs on Japan. Ever escalating their destructive capabilities, weaponry was measured in a frighteningly insane calculation: the number of times each could destroy the other with its arsenal.

Not since the days of Noah was mankind closer to destruction; never was the planet itself closer to annihilation. For almost fifty years, the American Eagle and the Russian Bear circled each other in a ring of death, each nation facing its foe in an unrelenting confrontation. The Cold War drained economies, people and patience.

It was difficult to imagine that there could ever be another way of life or a different, more rational world order. For those who are too young to remember, the Cold War was a time of abiding oppression upon all nations. There existed no solution, no wisdom, and no hope of resolution and reconciliation. From the ongoing confrontation in Berlin to the terrifying Cuban missile crisis, to the thousands of nuclear warheads poised in readiness to obliterate all life on planet earth, the only strategy was deterrence. Only the guarantee of nuclear retaliation and mutual annihilation kept the world from nuclear war.

Then, inexplicably and without warning, the Union of Soviet Socialist Republics began to unravel. Almost before our eyes, the nation disintegrated. Its fall was unprecedented. Never had so great and formidable a nation simply ceased to exist without either an assassination of its leadership or a sweeping civil war or revolt. Truly, there were no clearly observable outward signs of turmoil that indicated such drastic change was at hand.

The FBI and CIA were stunned; the news media were astounded; the prophetic teachers of Christendom, dumbfounded. Everyone had the USSR pegged; everyone was wrong. The sudden fall of the second most powerful nation in history was perfectly inconceivable. Yet it happened.

While military theorists, philosophers and politicians debate the various explanations on how the USSR collapsed, there were two results of its fall that were actually partial fulfillments of Scripture. First, the demise of the Soviet empire was orchestrated by the Lord to release the Russian Jews "from the land of the north" and restore them "to their own land" (Jer 16:14–16). Second, He desired to break the power of godless communism and thus open the Russian peoples to the gospel of Jesus Christ (Matt 24:14).

ONE SUPERPOWER UNDER GOD

There was a third outcome to the fall of the USSR which most of us, as Christians, have been slow to recognize or value. Simply, the death of the Soviet Union left one nation standing as leader of the world: the United States. America was not a battered foe, but triumphant; it had not been weakened by the conflict but, in many ways, actually strengthened.

Previously, at the end of WWII, Winston Churchill made an astute observation. He predicted that the world would follow "America's stride" into the future; increasingly, now, it is so.

It is important to remember: America is not an atheistic country, communistic, Hindu, Buddhist, Islamic or pagan; it has not descended into a "post-Christian" era, as have its European allies (though the standards of a large minority of U.S. Christians have slid). For whatever is wrong with America, it must be noted that the sole remaining superpower—the leading nation of the world—is also the most openly Christian.

In fact, in spite of its sin and obvious moral failures, since WWII America has remained the bastion of evangelical Christianity. This nation has been the primary launching pad of the most aggressive missionary outreach in the history of the world.

Let me quote Patrick Johnstone of the United Kingdom. He is considered by many to be the most respected compiler of statistical information on prayer and evangelism in Christianity. In his comprehensive resource book, *Operation World*, as an Englishman, he writes of America: *"No state in the world has been so strongly influenced by biblical Christianity."* [2]

SPIRITUAL WAR

I do not believe that the Cold War between the U.S. and Soviet Union was merely a military or cultural battle; at its deepest levels, it was a *spiritual* conflict. It was a war between a nation that recognized, to some degree, the influence and sovereignty of Christ versus a system whose

---

[2] *Operation World,* page 563

"state religion" was atheism, which vehemently opposed the very idea of God.

Indeed, America's national motto, though tested, remains *In God We Trust.* Every time there is a cash transaction in this nation, there is a witness to our spiritual heritage. For those with living faith, our motto remains an attainable vision for our future.

Atheists have challenged this motto often, taking it to the Supreme Court. Every time, their challenge has been unanimously rejected by both liberal and conservative judges alike.

A motto, according to Webster's dictionary, is a "guiding principle . . . a phrase expressing the spirit or purpose of an organization." A motto is an ideal more than an attainment. It's the standard toward which an organization charts its future, even while falling short of it.

More than half of all Americans sincerely consider the phrase, *In God We Trust,* as a true statement, reflective of their own lives. The trust expressed may not be a moment-by-moment reliance that the deeply spiritual possess; it may be true only in times of trouble, yet in times of trouble, eighty-five percent of Americans turn to God.

This maxim abides at the center of America's spiritual consciousness. Whether that ideal is wrapped in Methodist, Baptist or Pentecostal garments; whether it is expressed through high church liturgy or an inner city storefront, it is the guiding principle of the majority of Americans. We may disagree concerning *how* to worship, but most Christians in America agree concerning *Whom* we worship: We pay homage to the God of the Bible. To a large majority of Americans, the Lord is not only "God," but He is "Father" as well. He is the Supreme Being revealed in the New Testament, who sent His Son to die for our sins, to whom the majority of Americans look to in prayer.

You say, "Wait, the church in America is carnal, worldly. It's not New Testament Christianity." The first century church was far from perfect. They had divisions (see 1 Cor 1:11–12; Acts 15:37–39); immorality (see 1 Cor 5:1; Rev 2:18–21); leadership scandals (see 2 Tim 4:10); false doctrines (see Rev 2:14, 2:20); and dead churches (see Rev 3:1). Everything that we consider wrong with the church today was wrong then. They were imperfect Christians who turned their world upside down. God used flawed Christians then, and He is still doing so today.

I was born in 1946 and grew up during the Cold War. I still can recall times when, during the Sunday service, prayer was offered to God for Russia. It was ungarnished prayer, but sincere; simple, yet serious. Millions of average Americans were looking earnestly to God in prayer. I am fully convinced that when the Soviet Union collapsed in 1991, it was an answer to the countless moments of intercession that were offered to God from ordinary American people.

Yes, I'm sure people from many nations were also praying, including Russia itself. However, the essence of this conflict was between America, a nation whose motto was *In God We Trust,* versus a nation who categorically denied the existence of God, the USSR. The fact that Mikhail Gorbachev announced the dissolution of the Communist Party on December 25, 1991—the day we celebrate Christ's birth—is a profound witness that God was in America supporting His cause against atheism.

I am also convinced that when the USSR fell, a demonic stronghold that influenced much of the world also crumbled. In a real way, the dark "powers of the heavens" were beginning to experience the first of God's mighty end-time shakings (see Heb 12:26–27; Matt 24:29). As further evidence of this truth, consider: Since the fall of the Soviet empire, Christianity has harvested more souls worldwide than the *sum* of all previous centuries combined! The fact is, *since America became the last remaining superpower, the harvest of the nations has begun on a scale unprecedented in world history!*

WORKERS FROM EVERY NATION

I do not mean to imply that American Christianity has alone harvested these souls. No. In fact, in a few places Americans were not even involved. Men and women from many nations, together with the 60,000+ missionaries from the United States, have been sent by God to the uttermost parts of the world. Additionally, much of the harvest is occurring through the labors of Christian nationals, converts in foreign lands, whom the Holy Spirit has empowered to win their nations for Christ. We, in America, are participants with many others in the spreading of the gospel.

Still, the Lord has used the U.S., through its influence as world leader, to keep the nations open toward the biblical concepts of freedom, human rights and justice. This is not a little thing.

Before the fall of Soviet communism, the activity of the living church in Russia was small and embattled. Afterward, literally millions of people made confessions of faith and began their journey into salvation. Yes, the number of Christians can still increase during persecution, but it is also true that there are times when God must simply say, "Let My people go" (Ex 5:1), and the controlling powers of darkness are henceforth restrained from hindering the gospel.

THIS WAR IS NOT OVER

We said earlier that if America did not exist during World War II, we would be under the influence of Nazism. Furthermore, if America had not existed *since* World War II, Soviet communism (atheism) would have expanded virtually unchecked throughout the world. In both cases, it was primarily America (in league with its allies) that stood against these demonic philosophies. This, in turn, has increasingly opened the world for the spread of the gospel.

However, there are some who think American culture itself is a threat to the gospel. Certainly, in some ways, I agree. We have demonic strongholds in our own land that are a menace and must be brought down. If "freedom" is our virtue, it has also become our vice. For freedom has, for many, degenerated into lawlessness and license. As I mentioned in the preface, we have many things wrong with us as American Christians.

But, the idea that the U.S. must be destroyed so a purer Christianity can emerge is unfair for several reasons. First, condemning the United States is fatalistic and unbelieving in nature. Indeed, whatever is not of faith is sin (see Rom 14:23). Such thinking conveniently excuses the church from having to love, pray, fast, witness, and be involved as salt and light in the earth. Generally speaking, the attitude that America must be destroyed is the opinion of those whose love has grown cold (Matt 24:12); it is not the cry of those who care for America and are interceding for it.

In spite of predictions that America will spiritually and socially decline into irreversible darkness, the opposite is actually occurring. The incredible reduction of the crime rate (lowest since statistics began) reveals that something is happening in the United States as an answer to prayer. Abortion rates, divorce, teen pregnancies and people oppressed by poverty are all significantly dropping as well. Indeed, revival and renewal conditions, like the first drops of a summer thunderstorm, are breaking out in a number of churches.

We live in a time when ministries such as Mission America are bringing together large segments of the body of Christ for prayer. Scores of denominations and hundreds of prayer ministries are uniting, seeking God with fasting and prayer for revival in North America. Perhaps, for the first time in centuries, the church is not dividing, but is actually uniting around the Person of Christ.

I do not believe that Christ has inspired America's prayer movement only to ignore the prayers and then destroy us. There are millions of people praying fervently for the United States. A profound number of Christians are humbling themselves, praying and seeking the face of God like never before. So, even while we must acknowledge that America has major strongholds of sin, we have the encouragement from God Himself that He who began this good work will perfect it unto the day of Christ Jesus.

Yet, there is one more reason why, I believe, the United States is not about to be destroyed: America's role as the defender of freedom is not over. True, we no longer need to stand against Nazism or Soviet atheism, although the threat of communism is far from over. However, let us consider a future without the United States: In the hour of America's demise, radical Islamic extremists would begin their long-awaited Muslim holy war, Jihad, against all non-Muslims. In Asia the "Red Dragon," communist China, would begin the assimilation of the far east; and every ambitious, militaristic dictator would begin the brutalization of its weaker neighbor nations.

God's task for America is far from finished. In truth, it is just beginning. If the church continues to embrace Christlike intercession, not only will the Lord continue to reduce lawlessness in our cities, He will transform the soul of the United States and use this nation for the most glorious period of its history. Today, America does not stand at the brink of destruction, but at the threshold of its destiny.

CHAPTER ELEVEN

COMING OF AGE

The devil is trying to concentrate his efforts to bring [America] down morally, spiritually. Because he knows if he brings America down, there is probably no other nation in the world that will stand in his way. America is a main deterrent force against evil powers in the world today.

—*Dr. Thomas Wang (AD 2000 and Beyond)*

As an atheistic state, Russia's official stand was that there was no deity. God was a myth. Stalin taught that religion was merely the "opiate of the people." In fact, the Soviet communists mocked the reality of God. Their first cosmonauts bragged that they had flown to "heaven" and found no God there. Two generations of Russians were taught on every level of academia that God simply did not exist. The lie, "there is no God," saturated their society. Then the Lord spoke: *There is no Soviet Union.* Almost instantly the USSR vanished.

Its collapse was the most significant event since the end of World War II. Civilization is still rubbing its eyes, struggling to awaken to the reality in which it currently finds itself. It is as though mankind lived with a disease it thought terminal: nuclear war. The diagnosis has been changed and our condition is no longer terminal.

So, where do we go from here? Since 1991, everything about life on planet earth has changed. We no longer live beneath the shadow of nuclear death. You say, "I still think nuclear war will destroy the world." Well, you are welcome to live in whatever oppression you choose, but Jesus said plainly that, while we would hear of "wars and rumors of wars, do not be frightened . . . that is not yet the end" (Mark 13:7).

Yes, there may be nuclear bombs that fall into the hands of terrorists, and limited military conflicts will certainly involve us in the days ahead; but according to Christ, "war . . . is not . . . the end." So, if you are still afraid of nuclear annihilation even though Jesus commanded us, first, "do not be frightened," and secondly, that war will not destroy the earth, maybe you are being emotionally drained for nothing.

However, I don't want to minimize how difficult it has been for American Christians to accept that we have been given more time. We have had such an "end of the world" mentality. Some Christians are almost mad that their predictions about Russia, World War III, the fall of the United States, and the beginning of tribulation did not come to pass. Jeremiah said that he did not long for the mournful day. But sometimes I wonder if some of us are *disappointed* that the world hasn't been destroyed.

Since we are still alive and the world has not come to an end, we ought to finally come to terms with the fact that God has given us more time. Or maybe we always had more time, but we are just now discovering it. How much, only the Father knows, but we have time enough to rethink the short-term future and act in great boldness for the sake of the lost in the world.

So let's consider: In light of the Cold War's end, what principles shall guide and define the next millennium? As long as we remain on planet earth, the church needs to see itself seated at the table of world consciousness, drafting its role in shaping the world to come. Indeed, we have every right to be there. For, as we said, it was the influence of Christian values homogenized into American culture that God honored in toppling communism.

I believe that the 21st century, at least in the beginning, will continue extending the "American century." God has given this nation the position of worldwide influence. What we do with this responsibility, and why God is empowering the church at this strategic time, is central to our destiny.

You say, "God could get the gospel out by Himself. Nations do not need to be free to do so. Look at the church in the Roman Empire."

Yes, the early church was able to advance, and even flourish, in spite of persecution. But remember, Christians were only persecuted during various intervals. There were extended seasons when they were not oppressed by the Roman government.

Today, however, in nations where the gospel is outlawed or where Christians are tortured or jailed, there is a definite need for at least some freedom. Cultures must be opened somewhat before the gospel can expand.

Indeed, it is in this regard that I believe the Lord will continue to use America to keep doors opening in the otherwise closed cultures and societies of the world. The more openness these societies embrace, the greater the gospel can be proclaimed and received. Indeed, prior to the collapse of the Soviet Union, something unheard of in communist lands began to occur. The Russians called it *glasnost.* It means "openness." Worldwide, openness is what the influence of America provides.

CHAPTER TWELVE

IS THE UNITED STATES IN THE BIBLE?

S o, if the Lord's immediate plans are not to destroy America, then what is in God's heart for this nation? Is there anything in the Scriptures about the United States upon which our faith can rest? The Bible has a number of general promises that we can apply to our land. These, though they lack clear or specific references to the United States, still supply a foundation for our faith. Isaiah 60:1–3 is such a text. It reads:

> Arise, shine; for your light has come, and the glory of the Lord has risen upon you. For behold, darkness will cover the earth, and deep darkness the peoples; but the Lord will rise upon you, and His glory will appear upon you. And nations will come to your light, and kings to the brightness of your rising.

Think of it! Nations and kings will come to the glory of Christ arising in the church! Regardless of where on earth you currently live or how dark the world is around you, this text is a living promise to all who pray for their nation!

Personally, I have stood upon this word often, especially in the face of America's spiritual darkness, when doubts would creep in and I'd wonder if all effort was too late. Isaiah assures us that, if God's glory rises upon us, even in the midst of deep darkness over the people, nations will come to our light. [3]

But, you say, America is too rebellious, too unrestrained. The Second Psalm gives us encouragement to persevere in prayer when it seems governments are casting away the cords and fetters of godly, moral restraint (see Ps 2:3). In the face of the world's rebellion, the Lord says, "Ask of Me, and I will surely give the nations as Thine inheritance, and the *very* ends of the earth as Thy possession" (Ps 2:8).

There are many other Scriptures that call us to pray and believe for a national awakening (Isa 52:15; Ps 67:4; etc.). But I want to submit a text to you that may, indeed, specifically refer to God's plan for America in the days ahead.

THE EAGLE'S WINGS

The Scriptures speak of a time when great persecution will break out at the end of the age. In the midst of this persecution, we read an arresting message in Rev 12:14. It says:

And the two wings of the great eagle were given to the woman, in order that she might fly into the

---

[3] See *The Days of His Presence* for further information.

wilderness to her place, where she was nourished for a time and times and half a time, from the presence of the serpent.

The book of Revelation is, by definition, a book of revelations. Its symbolic portraits must be interpreted not only in historic terms but also in light of end-time realities. Frankly, no one has accurately been able to interpret this book to the satisfaction of everyone else. It would be a sin of bold presumption on my part to assume I am the first to present an infallible interpretation. Even as we seek to stay humble, let us cautiously proceed, relying on God and time itself to confirm His Word. In that attitude, let me submit to you my thoughts.

The above Scripture speaks of the wings of the great eagle being given to the woman. The woman is not a singular individual, but a symbol of the holy, praying church, pregnant to give birth to its end-time elect (see Matthew Henry's Commentary on Rev 12:1–11). Amidst great spiritual warfare, she delivers her child, who in turn is caught up to God (Rev 12:5). Some interpret the woman to be unsaved Israel giving birth to Christ, but this cannot be, for the woman overcomes her conflict with the dragon by the "blood of the Lamb" (Rev 12:11). Therefore, since she trusts Christ, she must symbolize the true, glorious Church, those who hold "the testimony of Jesus" (Rev 12:17).

Just as the woman represents a holy people, so the "wings of the great eagle" depict a provision from God that secures for the woman refuge from the rage of the evil one. The eagle symbolizes something which is capable of providing protection from what would otherwise be a worldwide persecution of Christians by the dragon.

I submit to you that this reference to a "great eagle" could very easily be a prophetic portrait of the United States of America. Before you dismiss such an idea, consider: There simply has never been in the history of the world a nation more committed to being a refuge for persecuted people than America. Additionally, when we consider that the national symbol of the U.S. *is* the "great eagle," the symbolism becomes even more plausible.

It is this defense of freedom, as well as the American ideal of protecting human rights, that is central to what it means to be an American.[4] Indeed, many of those who originally came to America did so while fleeing persecution for their faith. In a real way, this Scripture has *already* been fulfilled by many of our founding fathers. The persecution our forefathers suffered was sown, like a seed, into the DNA of American culture. Protection for persecuted people, from God's view, has always been at the center of America's historic purpose.

To provide shelter to persecuted people is still central to our ideals today. Since God provided the great eagle to symbolize protection of persecuted Christians at the end of the age, and since it is also the symbol of America, we ought not to abandon ourselves to a hopeless view of the future. It is in our compelling interest to pray that America would continue to be a place of provision and protection right up until the rapture of the church.

---

[4] See appendix, The Statue of Liberty, for additional insight on America's role.

CHAPTER THIRTEEN

THE SECRET TO NATIONAL PROSPERITY

For whatever ungodly conditions remain in the U.S., there are two biblical mandates America *does* obey that are fundamental to its economy and prosperity. I refer to them as "secrets" because, as Christians, we often speak of our nation as though it was completely without virtue.

I personally have felt the Lord's displeasure whenever I murmur or complain. After I repent for ingratitude, it is amazing how I am lifted above my circumstances; they are not as dark as they first appeared. Indeed, I actually can see what God is doing when I begin my intercession with thanksgiving.

So, even as we mourn for America's sins, we must also remain thankful to God for its virtues. It is not enough that we doctrinally know the truth of God if our attitudes contradict that knowledge. Thus, Paul warns,

> For even though they knew God, they did not honor Him as God, or give thanks; but they became futile in their speculations, and their foolish heart was darkened.　　—Rom 1:21

To pray without giving thanks dishonors God; it opens the door to futility, and darkens our heart's capacity to see the Lord and the blessings He has bestowed. Indeed, an unthankful heart is a grumbling heart, which makes our lives vulnerable to be "destroyed by the destroyer" (1 Cor 10:10). I have a Swedish friend, Lars Enarson, who taught me a great truth. He said, "Thanksgiving is the language of faith." Jesus prayed with thanksgiving (see John 11:41; Mark 8:6); Paul taught that we should always pray "with thanksgiving" (Phil 4:6). Ingratitude is a major stronghold in the church in America. We need to repent of it if we will truly fulfill God's will (see 1 Thess 5:18).

So, what has America been doing right that, according to God's Word, carries the promise of economic well-being? First, the United States is a giving nation. In fact, in the history of mankind there simply has never been a nation more charitable to other nations.

I know that a number of my colleagues are predicting divine wrath upon America's economy, but I would ask them to rethink or consider prayerfully the words of Jesus concerning the principle of giving. He said,

> Give, and it will be given to you; good measure, pressed down, shaken together, running over, they will pour into your lap. For by your standard of measure it will be measured to you in return.
>
> —Luke 6:38

The United States has cast its bread upon many waters and, economically and relationally, it is being returned to us. Think about it: when was there a calamity anywhere in the world where the suffering people were not helped by American hands, resources and finances? In fact, as the news breaks of a major disaster, American charitable agencies kick into action. Within hours, volunteers are at the scene and within days millions of dollars pour toward the need.

Here is an excerpt of a letter from a professor in Wisconsin. He wrote in response to the first two chapters of this book, which were published beforehand in our newsletter. He writes,

A doctor from a Rotary Club at the University of Minnesota was reporting on a project in Chile which his club and mine have jointly sponsored. We have been helping a school for deaf children with needed equipment, from school supplies and playground equipment to modern hearing aids which have been donated by a local manufacturer, Starkey Labs. At the end of his slides showing the school and the kids wearing their new hearing aids, he showed a picture of an older man. He said, "This man is originally from France. He told me that any place in the world that you see people from one country reaching out to help other countries, the Americans are behind it."

The amazing thing is that, for Americans, it does not take much coaxing to reach out and help. As soon as we hear of suffering people somewhere, we are looking for a way to respond. In fact, the president and chief executive officer of the national Council on Foundations, Dorothy Ridings, stated, "American giving to churches, foundations and other groups, is so phenomenal that this is being called the golden age of philanthropy" (*Cedar Rapids Gazette, April 10, 1999*).

God sees the suffering of mankind. Because of His great love, the Lord is touched by human tragedy, whether the suffering is in Africa or Central America, Kosovo or

North Korea. In very real ways Americans seek to alleviate this sorrow among all peoples (see Judges 10:16; Heb 4:15 AMPLIFIED).

Again, God promises,

> He who is gracious to a poor man lends to the Lord, and He will repay him for his good deed.
>
> —Prov 19:17

I believe a certain measure of American economic strength is attached to the generosity of this nation toward others. It is a blessing upon our land.

THE JEWISH CONNECTION

There is a T-shirt sold in the Holy Land that reads, "Don't worry, America, Israel is right behind you." There is a special friendship that exists between America and Israel that is unique in all the world. America has been especially generous and compassionate toward Israel. In fact, no nation in the history of the world has stood with Israel as we have over the last half century.

To understand what this means to God, we must look at His promise to Abraham:

> Now the Lord said to Abram, "Go forth from your country, and from your relatives and from your father's house, to the land which I will show you;
>
> "And I will make you a great nation, and I will bless you, and make your name great; and so you shall be a blessing; and I will bless those who bless you, and the one who curses you I will

curse. And in you all the families of the earth
shall be blessed."   —Gen 12:1–3

In the very first promise that the Lord gave to Abraham, He provided a means for all nations to receive and sustain divine blessings. He said, "I will bless those who bless you, and the one who curses you I will curse."

This promise was not limited to Abraham, but it was passed on to Isaac and then to Jacob, to whom the Lord gave the name, *Israel*. In the Old Testament, Balaam prophesied under divine inspiration. He said of Israel, "Blessed is everyone who blesses you, and cursed is everyone who curses you" (Num 24:9).

Today, the people of Israel have inherited a most unique position among all nations: their origin can be tracked directly to an encounter with God. Israel's historic relationship with the Almighty makes the Jews a symbol, a unique possession, of God in the earth. The Lord has dwelt in their midst. From their beginning the Jews have been a people called by God unto Himself. The word *holy* means "set apart for God." As such, Israel, its land, and its destiny are holy, or "set apart" to the Lord. The people yet need revival. There is much need of prayer and support, but the God who brought them back will also raise them up.

Israel's relationship with America

According to former Prime Minister Benjamin Netanyahu, there has "never been in Israel's long history a friend like the U.S." *(speech welcoming President Clinton to Israel, Fall 1998)*. This is quite an endorsement, and it is true: America has been the most faithful, absolutely the strongest, and by far the most generous friend Israel has ever had.

As we said earlier, if there had been no U.S., there would be no Israel. The Jewish state has grown and become stable and is now prospering because God has used American strength and generosity. Indeed, the very fact that Israel has survived is because it grew up under the shelter of American friendship and commitment *(see appendix for comments from various presidents concerning the Jews and Israel).*

Israel receives more foreign aid from the U.S. than any nation, currently over five billion dollars a year. Additionally, it receives several billions of dollars annually in charitable contributions from North America and Europe but, again, the biggest donor nation is America.

Remember what the Lord told Abraham? "I will bless those who bless you." It was only a few years ago that the deficit was climbing to over five trillion dollars; now the U.S. has to decide what to do with its annual surpluses. America has been blessed with the strongest economy in the world, and nations throughout the world use the U.S. dollar as a secondary currency. To have a stable economy is not a sin. It is a blessing.

Yet, good people keep predicting the collapse and death of the American economy. It is true that the Lord will withhold certain appointed blessings if there is sin in other areas of our lives, so we must proceed with humility and the fear of the Lord.

But I want to add another observation concerning Israel and the United States. I call this an observation, but it is more the awareness of a supernatural mystery surrounding the relationship between Israel and America. It is something holy that is attached to our mutual destiny.

Since WWII, there has been a parallel between the United States and Israel. Both have risen together into the forefront of human affairs; both have deep spiritual roots in the God of the Bible. I feel, somehow, as revival comes to America it will not only touch the world; it will also birth the moving of God in Israel.

> For I do not want you, brethren, to be uninformed of this mystery, lest you be wise in your own estimation, that a partial hardening has happened to Israel until the fulness of the Gentiles has come in; and thus all Israel will be saved.
>
> —Rom 11:25–26

Listen to this thought: "a partial hardening has happened to Israel until the fulness of the Gentiles has come in." God's plan for Israel is activated after the fulness of the Gentiles come to Christ. The entire sequence of end-time events stands in the wings waiting for the fulness of the Gentile harvest—and America in revival is key to this worldwide ingathering.

ONE MORE THOUGHT

Besides America's charitable side toward the needy of the world and Israel, there is one other consideration. The economic stability of the nation has run parallel with the emergence of the prayer movement. The Scriptures tell us, "By the blessing of the upright a city is exalted, but by the mouth of the wicked it is torn down" (Prov 11:11).

Since the church has begun to bless America's cities, and pray for this nation and its leaders, we have seen the blessing of the Lord return upon us. I realize that economic conditions run in cycles and that, at the time of this writing, we are at the peak of growth. This could all change tomorrow, and will certainly be adjusted and shaken by the global effects of the Y2K problem. However, the words that experts are currently using to describe America's economy are all superlatives: "phenomenal," "extraordinary," "unprecedented," to name a few.

I don't think we realize the impact that the prayer movement has had on bringing change to the world. We are seeing so many areas transformed in our society: the statistics for crime, abortion, divorce and sexually active teens are lowering; God is doing a great work. It is also inevitable that there will be tremors in the financial sector of the world. However, for as long as we continue giving to oppressed peoples, particularly Israel, I think America's economy will continue to be resurgent and strong for the near future.

CHAPTER FOURTEEN

A WORLD
IN REVIVAL
AND HARVEST

W e began this book by asking you to consider what the civilized world would be like without the United States. Now, I'm going to ask you to consider a world with America in revival. I do not mean a revival merely of emotional religion, but a deep revival, born of genuine Christlikeness in the church. Picture America experiencing a Christ awakening, where a priesthood of mature believers join the Lamb before the throne of God's grace; where the Lamb is offered as sacrifice for America's sin, God receives the sacrifice and, according to 2 Chronicles 7:14, He heals our land.

Picture a repentant America touching Islamic, Hindu and Buddhist peoples with the love of Jesus. Picture a holy America where our movies have moral, Christ-inspired lessons and where the message of redemption is played out in a myriad of ways around the world. Envision a million praying, loving missionaries, empowered by the Holy

Spirit to heal and encourage nations on every level of society.

We can go the way of the judgmental and critical. We can listen to those without vision who seek to pull America down, like Samson, upon themselves and their enemies. Or, we can become Christlike and see a true golden age come to this land. Think of it, my friend, can you envision a world where the most powerful nation on earth has become the most godly?

Do not say this cannot happen. Remember, God is not looking impatiently at His watch, He's listening to His heart. He takes no pleasure in the death of the wicked; He desires for all men to be saved (2 Pet 3:9) and has made provision for all men at the cross (2 Cor 5:21). He inspired revival before. He can do it again.

Do you remember the story of the demonized boy whose father pleaded with Jesus for help? The man approached Christ feeling defeated, almost hopeless, weary with fighting to keep the boy alive after repeated demonic attacks. The man asked Jesus, "If You can do anything, take pity on us and help us!" (Mark 9:22)

Our attitude is often like that of this man. Our shoulders are hunched from fasting and we are wearied with the fight to keep America alive. We come to the Lord looking for pity instead of power; we're seeking comfort instead of conviction to take a stand for America.

To ask for mere pity from a God who has given us "everything pertaining to life and godliness" is an insult (2 Pet 1:3). Jesus retorted, "If You can! All things are possible to him who believes" (Mark 9:23).

ALL THINGS ARE POSSIBLE!

Let Christ's words become our battle cry. "With God," Jesus said, "all things are possible" (Matt 19:26). Lay aside the weight of unbelief; there is a race to be run and we can win it. Ask God for more love, for love believes all things, hopes all things and endures all things.

We are in the season of the miraculous. Who would have thought beforehand that the USSR would fall and millions would come to Christ in that nation? Who would have predicted that *hundreds of millions* would have come to Christ just in the last ten years? Who would have thought after listening to those who said America was doomed that we would see major decreases in crime, divorce, abortion, and teen pregnancy?

Today, there is a resurgence of moral values on college campuses around America. Did we expect this good news? Did we anticipate that a deep and wonderful revival would hit the sports world so that hundreds of Christian athletes would become role models for our youth or that whole teams would huddle together in public prayer after games?

Who saw ten years ago that the church would be uniting in prayer? Or that reconciliation between races and denominations would begin in earnest? Or that a million and a half men would stand in repentance for America at the national capitol?

Daniel said, "The people who know their God will display strength and take action" (Dan 11:32). He went on to say, "Those who have insight will shine brightly like the brightness of the expanse of heaven, and those who lead the many to righteousness, like the stars forever and ever" (Dan 12:3). It is not a time for fear, but faith. We do not need to come beggarly to Christ for pity; He is extending to us His power through our prayers, as long as we don't give up.

Have you heard the story of the man who was driving home from work one day and stopped to watch a local Little League baseball game in a park near his home? He sat down behind the bench on the first baseline and asked one of the boys what the score was.

"We're behind 14 to nothing," the little boy answered with a smile.

"Really," he said. "I have to say you don't look very discouraged."

"Discouraged," the boy asked with a puzzled look on his face, "why should we be discouraged? We haven't been up to bat yet."

It is not time to be discouraged. I believe the devil has run up the score, but really, we haven't been to bat yet. For much of the past thirty years, we have been playing a poor defense to the devil's initiatives (some of us weren't even playing, but sitting quietly on the bench). But, my friends, the devil's turn is nearly over, the church is getting ready to step up to the batter's box.

The Columbine tragedy in Littleton, Colo., was going to be one of the devil's last runs. Instead, God turned it into a home run for heaven, with *millions* hearing the good news proclaimed through CNN's live coverage of the funeral services of the martyred Christian kids. Can you see how God is softening America's heart?

Good things are happening all around us. America is going to experience the greatest Christ-awakening in its history. I make no apologies for believing as I do. Even if our country briefly turns darker spiritually, I am fully convinced that America will return to God's light. Yes, even now, America stands at the threshold of destiny.

Questions and Answers

You keep saying America will have peace and there will be safety here. How does that fit with Paul's warning in 1 Thessalonians?

First of all, I have never said America will perpetually enjoy peace and safety, as though there will not be earthquakes, storms, economic pressures or unforeseen world conflicts that we will face. I am saying if the church stays true to its destiny, which is to reveal the nature of Christ, then God will bring America into its destiny: revival and participation in worldwide harvest.

Currently, we enjoy an increasing sense of stability here, but it is a relatively unique situation. God has been answering prayer and America is slowly turning around. But let's look at the verse where Paul speaks of this false peace that will companion the antichrist and his worldwide influence over mankind. The apostle warns,

> While they are saying, "Peace and safety!" then destruction will come upon them suddenly like birth pangs upon a woman with child; and they shall not escape.
>
> —1 Thess 5:3

Paul warns that the world, not just one nation, would enter a time of relief from conflict. The whole world is not enjoying peace and safety. There are many nations that would love to enjoy a little "peace and safety" for awhile. Do you think Russia, Africa, Israel, Japan, Greece, Ireland, Serbia, Turkey, Korea, Iran, India, Brazil, Malaysia, and scores of other troubled nations are saying or experiencing unusual "peace and safety"?

We shouldn't superimpose our short-term prosperity onto the whole world nor view peace as a sign of imminent doom. There is nothing wrong with peace or safety. When the Bible warns of the world attaining a false sense of relief, it is in context with the manifestation of the antichrist and his universal government. It involves receiving a certain visible mark on the forehead or hand. The antichrist will exalt himself above every god or so-called object of worship while actually sitting in the temple in Jerusalem and displaying himself as God (see 2 Thess 2).

However, there currently is no temple in Jerusalem and no antichrist bringing the world together. So, we must conclude that if the Lord gave us warning signs to discern the times, we are *not* in the era of the antichrist. It is my opinion that we should keep tithing and enjoy the blessing of the Lord, temporal as it is. Let us not confuse our day with what will happen when the antichrist assumes his worldwide role of spiritual/political leader. This is not that which is to come.

You call the church to pray, but America is so sinful I feel like the Lord is telling me what He told Jeremiah, to not pray for this nation (see Jer 14:11).

Well, He also told Jeremiah to "roam to and fro through the streets of Jerusalem, and look . . . if there is one who does justice, who seeks truth, then I will pardon her" (Jer 5:1). It is easy to slot ourselves into a couple references in the Bible where the Lord says, "don't pray," and ignore the *hundreds* of verses that call for prayer and involvement. Personally, when I hear people quote what the Lord told Jeremiah as an excuse to condemn America, I feel it is a cop-out. Listen carefully, God has not raised up millions of intercessors to tell them not to pray. He has inspired the prayer movement because He intends to answer our prayers.

The fact is, even after the Lord told Jeremiah to stop praying for the nation, the prophet continued praying. The Lord told Moses, "Now then let Me alone," so He could destroy Israel, but Moses refused (Ex 32:10–13). By persisting, he soon caused the Lord to "change His mind" concerning destruction (Ex 32:14). To continue praying when told not to pray is the only time direct disobedience pleases the Almighty.

I feel America's economy is going to come under God's wrath and that there is going to be a major stock market crash.

Well, I'm not a stockbroker or the son of a stockbroker, but market crashes are inevitable. If you want to take some or all of your money out, you might be wise to do so. But, I do not believe the wrath of God is coming on this nation (any more than it already has in the form of judgments upon lawlessness and sin). Without a doubt, we will pass through economic swings in the near future, just as we have in the past. My advice is to keep giving, use common sense, and don't become fearful. If you ask your grandparents what to do, you will probably make it through anything we will face economically in the days ahead.

Here's what I believe: we have an economy in the kingdom of God which neither moth nor rust can corrupt (Matt 6:20). If our treasures are truly in heaven, and we seek first for God's kingdom on earth, Jesus assures us that whatever we need will be provided us.

An interesting side note: After the Lord spoke repeatedly through Jeremiah of the upcoming exile of the Jews, He then told him to buy property—to *invest* in Israel—even though they would go through judgment (Jer 32). There may be a market crash or a "correction" ahead, but I'm still investing my *love* and *prayers* in America.

America has abandoned Israel to favor the PLO. Don't you think God will judge the United States for that?

America has not abandoned its support of Israel, but politically I can understand why American diplomacy seeks to create a dialogue between Israel and the PLO. Indeed, the Palestinians have legitimate needs. They are an extremely oppressed people who will never quietly go away on their own no matter how nicely Israel asks them. So these two groups need to talk.

No one knows how God will supernaturally fulfill His promises to Israel. However, I agree with those who say, on a human scale, there is no clear answer among men. What America seeks to accomplish is to keep both sides talking, for as long as they are talking they are usually not warring. I think the United States sincerely seeks to find some kind of solution for the Palestinians. We know that unless a people have hope that their situation can change through normal means, they will otherwise seek change through violent means.

However, it is here, as I understand this crisis, where we must intercede most intensely. For the PLO has not only desired statehood, it wants Jerusalem for its capitol! Israel would never consider losing their ancient capitol, and the idea of Palestinian statehood is an encroachment the Jews are not willing to bear. God have mercy!

Personally, I have very little faith that any peace brokered between the Israelis and the PLO will provide a permanent solution. Still, political solutions and compromises do provide something almost as important as real peace; they give both sides "time." As long as both factions are talking, they are not shooting, and this is not a little thing.

Of course, we must continue in our posture of prayer for Israel, the Palestinians and the U.S. as well. Whatever God does in restoring the Jews to Himself will be key in their reconciliation with the Arabs as well. And all of this will come through the prayers of the saints.

Israel has never had to rely on another nation before. Is America taking the place of God?

Historically, when Israel was right with God, He defended the nation against its enemies. There were, however, times when the Lord used major empires to protect the Jews, such as Persia under Cyrus and Ahasuerus, and Rome during the Maccabees. On these occasions, the benevolence of these mighty empires toward Israel was a tool in God's hand and, with Cyrus at least, used to fulfill Scripture.

The American government, its schools and its systems are corrupt throughout. We need to pull our people out and "be separate."

Jesus said, "as the Father has sent me, I also send you" (John 20:21). You and I are not to be *hidden* somewhere, but *sent* somewhere. I can understand parents not wanting their children to be taught in public schools, but beyond that I draw the line. We are not Essenes or monks. Though we are not *of* the world, we are sent *to* the world as ambassadors for Christ (2 Cor 5:20).

Frankly, it has always bothered me that Christians would evacuate key positions in government and society. When Satan tempted Jesus with the world and its glory, he said, "I will give You all this domain and its glory; for it has been handed over to me" (Luke 4:6). God did not hand the world over to the devil, *man did.* And we are doing the same thing when we abdicate our positions of authority. After we turn over key leadership positions to the world, we then condemn non-Christians for not doing God's will! We ask God to judge them for their sin, but we have sinned ourselves because we stopped being salt and light to the world (Matt 5:13–15). Jesus said: "Behold, I send you out as sheep in the midst of wolves; therefore be shrewd as serpents, and innocent as doves" (Matt 10:16).

So I disagree with abandoning the systems of the world. That is the reason we are in the situation we've been in for the past thirty years. We need to be in the world, but not of it. We need Christian politicians, teachers, lawyers, news reporters, policemen, and judges. These are ministry posts that are no less a calling than being a pastor or missionary.

I tend to be a "prophetic" type person. I agree with what you say, but don't we still need to speak the judgments of God against sinners?

Yes. But we don't want to model our lives after Old Testament prophets; our pattern is Jesus Christ. There is, and will always be, the need to speak the judgments of God against sin. Jesus did this against Jerusalem, but He also spent time there, loving the people, healing and teaching. He wept over the city. And, He was probably looking at Jerusalem when He prayed, "Father forgive them." The judgment He spoke was out of a broken heart, not an angry spirit.

So our pattern is Christ. Yet, it is true that in the body of Christ God has people with a "prophetic gifting" or personality. They tend to abhor what they feel is evil and cling to what they see as good. Because of this they may make quick judgments.

Their primary concern is stopping the spread of evil and their desire is for justice and truth to prevail. This at times can lead to exposing the sinner rather than looking to restore the sinner. The prophet sees life as either right or wrong. They are also not a "respecter of persons" but apply the same standards to themselves, thereby being extremely self-critical.

People who only move in mercy need the prophetic perspective. The "mercy" motivated individual can best be summarized as able to empathize with hurting people. These people have a deep understanding of others who are going through mental and emotional distress. They are deeply loyal to friends even to the point of taking up offenses of those being hurt. If they do not use spiritual discernment as to why there is suffering, they may give sympathy to those who are suffering as a direct result of violating God's moral laws. In the body of Christ, both personalities are called to submit to one another and balance each other's perspective.

What about abortion? Don't you feel God is angry at America because of the nearly thirty-million abortions since 1971?

Yes. I am angry myself every time I think of this and I must turn my anger to prayer. I am sure the Lord is grieved over this crime, especially over the hardness of our hearts concerning late-term abortion. These are terrible sins. But, I think we need to remember that the Lord also sees the big picture. He sees we are, perhaps, only an election away from reversing Roe vs. Wade. He knows that nearly half of all Americans oppose legalized abortion and over sixty percent would vote to end late-term abortions. Additionally, more than three-fourths of all Americans believe abortion should be either outlawed or allowed only under limited circumstances (Gallup Poll).

Currently, the numbers are increasingly pro-life in this nation, and abortion itself is at its lowest ebb since 1975. If we do not give up, and if we are willing to see victory come in stages, we may soon realize the end to legalized abortion. Imagine if abortion were outlawed here, what a statement that would make to the rest of the free world!

Here is why I believe we will win the war over abortion: The concept of protecting basic human rights is an irreversible drive in the corporate American psyche. Indeed, it is encoded into our concept of self-awareness as Americans and is the summary thought in our Declaration of Independence. We base all our other freedoms on the principle that "all men were endowed by their Creator with certain inalienable rights."

For those who came from Africa, the long battle for equal rights had to be fought, but it was the Law itself that stood on the side of people of color in their struggle. Whether it is true or not, we have come to believe about ourselves that, as Americans, we represent the world's standard for human rights issues; whether those rights involve minorities, women, consumers, workers or even animals and trees. So abortion is a contradiction in the steady stream of American consciousness, and more and more people are seeing it as so.

That is why I believe that it is only a matter of time until this injustice shall be overturned both by law and by popular demand in this nation. Until then, we must continue to stand in intercession before God, and we must work to legally change the laws of our local communities.

What are your views about Y2K?

Some folks are convinced the year 2000 will trigger the end of the world. Others feel that it will cause major energy-related problems, especially in the national power grid, which will lead to riots, insurrection, and the breakdown of society as we know it. Others simply yawn and go their way, convinced that those who yell, *"the sky is falling,"* have been wrong before.

The fact is, no one knows what will happen. But my experience with the Lord and prayer is that, if we increase our prayer for America during the months prior to the year 2000, God will minimize the consequences of this problem and turn them into opportunities for His glory. Just as prayer for our cities has resulted in criminals being captured and violence decreasing, so prayer can result in glitches being located and computer systems being fixed quickly.

As far as practical things, my family is preparing for two to three weeks of disruption.

The Statue of Liberty

Let me quote part of the poem that's on the Statue of Liberty:

> *"Keep, ancient lands, your storied pomp!"*
> *cries she with silent lips.*
> *Give me your tired, your poor,*
> *your huddled masses yearning to breathe free;*
> *The wretched refuse of your teeming shore.*
> *Send these, the homeless, tempest-tossed to me,*
> *I lift my lamp beside the golden door.*
> *—by Emma Lazarus, New York City, 1883*

The Statue of Liberty was originally called Liberty Enlightening the World, symbolizing liberty in the form of a woman wearing flowing robes and a spiked crown of seven spokes (symbolizing the seven oceans and the seven continents) who holds a torch aloft in her right hand and carries in her left a book of law inscribed "July 4, 1776." The broken chains, symbolizing the overthrow of tyranny, lie at her feet. Originally it was given as a gift from France, conceived as a gesture of international friendship. Immigrants the world over would see "Liberty" welcoming them to America's shores. For more than one hundred years the Statue of Liberty has become the global symbol of freedom.[5]

A further note on chapter eleven: Referring back to our text in Revelation, it is significant that the Holy Spirit does not actually refer simply to "the wings of the great eagle," but specifically "the *two* wings." Perhaps this is just a literary device to emphasize some unknown truth. Or, it may actually have further significance. Is it possible that the Holy Spirit is making a distinction between the "two wings" of the eagle, just as there is a distinction between the "Left Wing" and the "Right Wing" of the American government? Is the Lord assuring us that, during the time of persecution, both governing political philosophies would agree concerning its role of protection?

---

[5] Taken from the Statue of Liberty State Park Web site at
http://www.libertystatepark.com/statueof.htm

In that sense, the Scripture becomes clearer: The *two* wings of the great eagle would give even more detail on how we ought to pray.

Indeed, in America today we divide politically: white evangelicals generally vote Republican, while black evangelicals look to the Democrats. For the most part, each segment of the church is drawn to the biblical precepts they see represented in the respective parties. Christians who vote Republican do so primarily for the anti-abortion stand; Christians who vote for the Democrats are more conscious of the need to care for the poor and hurting of our nation. God needs Christians in both parties to be salt and light and to balance the influence of the world in our government. I personally like to think that God would give the "two wings of the great eagle" to the woman.

If you have a different view concerning this verse, remember I am not dogmatic about this interpretation.

However, no one can deny America's historic openness and protection toward the persecuted people of the world. My faith says that this role of protection will continue to be one of the principal redeeming qualities of this nation right into the very time of the end.

Views of U.S. Presidents Toward Israel

At the web site http://www.us-israel.org/jsource/ustoc.html were the following quotes by various American presidents concerning America's relationship with Israel.

HISTORIC COMMITMENT; FUTURE BLESSING

John Adams: I will insist that the Hebrews have done more to civilize man than any other nation. *(Letter to Thomas Jefferson)*

John Quincy Adams: [I believe in the] rebuilding of Judea as an independent nation. *(Letter to Major Mordecai Manuel Noah)*

Abraham Lincoln: Not long after the Emancipation Proclamation, President Abraham Lincoln met a Canadian Christian Zionist, Henry Wentworth Monk, who expressed hope that Jews who were suffering oppression in Russia and Turkey be emancipated "by restoring them to their national home in Palestine." Lincoln said this was "a noble dream and one shared by many Americans." The President said his chiropodist was a Jew who "has so many times 'put me upon my feet' that I would have no objection to giving his countrymen 'a leg up.'"

Woodrow Wilson: The allied nations with the fullest concurrence of our government and people are agreed that in Palestine shall be laid the foundations of a Jewish Commonwealth. *(Reaction to the Balfour Declaration)*

Recalling the previous experiences of the colonists in applying the Mosaic Code to the order of their internal life, it is not to be wondered at that the various passages in the Bible that serve to undermine royal authority, stripping the Crown of its cloak of divinity, held up before the pioneer Americans the Hebrew Commonwealth as a model government. In the spirit and essence of our Constitution, the influence of the Hebrew Commonwealth was paramount in that it was not only the highest authority for the principle, "that rebellion to tyrants is obedience to God," but also because it was in itself a divine precedent for a pure democracy, as distinguished from monarchy, aristocracy or any other form of government.

Warren Harding: It is impossible for one who has studied at all the services of the Hebrew people to avoid the faith that they will one day be restored to their historic national home and there enter on a new and yet greater phase of their contribution to the advance of humanity.

Calvin Coolidge: Coolidge expressed his "sympathy with the deep and intense longing which finds such fine expression in the Jewish National Homeland in Palestine."

The Jews themselves, of whom a considerable number were already scattered throughout the colonies, were true to the teachings of their prophets. The Jewish faith is predominantly the faith of liberty.

Herbert Hoover: Palestine which, desolate for centuries, is now renewing its youth and vitality through enthusiasm, hard work, and self-sacrifice of the Jewish pioneers who toil there in a spirit of peace and social justice.

Harry Truman: I had faith in Israel before it was established, I have faith in it now. *(Granting de facto recognition to the new Jewish State—eleven minutes after Israel's proclamation of independence)*

I believe it has a glorious future before it—not just another sovereign nation, but as an embodiment of the great ideals of our civilization. *(May 26, 1952)*

Dwight D. Eisenhower: Our forces saved the remnant of the Jewish people of Europe for a new life and a new hope in the reborn land of Israel. Along with all men of good will, I salute the young state and wish it well.

John Kennedy: This nation, from the time of President Woodrow Wilson, has established and continued a tradition of friendship with Israel because we are committed to all free societies that seek a path to peace and honor individual right. In the prophetic spirit of Zionism all free men today look to a better world and in the experience of Zionism we know that it takes courage and perseverance and dedication to achieve it.

Israel was not created in order to disappear—Israel will endure and flourish. It is the child of hope and home of the brave. It can neither be broken by adversity nor demoralized by success. It carries the shield of democracy and it honors the sword of freedom.

Lyndon Johnson: The United States and Israel share many common objectives . . . chief of which is the building of a better world in which every nation can develop its resources and develop them in freedom and peace.

Our society is illuminated by the spiritual insights of the Hebrew prophets. America and Israel have a common love of human freedom and they have a common faith in a democratic way of life.

Most if not all of you have very deep ties with the land and with the people of Israel, as I do, for my Christian faith sprang from yours. . . . The Bible stories are woven into my childhood memories as the gallant struggle of modern Jews to be free of persecution is also woven into our souls. *(Speech before B'nai B'rith)*

When Soviet Premier Aleksei Kosygin asked Johnson why the United States supports Israel when there are eighty million Arabs and only three million Israelis, the President replied simply: "Because it is right."

Richard Nixon: Nixon asserted that the United States stands by its friends and that "Israel is one of its friends."

Americans admire a people who can scratch a desert and produce a garden. The Israelis have shown qualities that Americans identify with: guts, patriotism, idealism, a passion for freedom. I have seen it. I know. I believe that.

Gerald Ford: [The American] commitment to the security and future of Israel is based upon basic morality as well as enlightened self-interest. Our role in supporting Israel honors our own heritage.

Jimmy Carter: The United States . . . has a warm and a unique relationship of friendship with Israel that is morally right. It is compatible with our deepest religious convictions, and it is right in terms of America's own strategic interests. We are committed to Israel's security, prosperity, and future as a land that has so much to offer the world.

The survival of Israel is not just a political issue, it is a moral imperative. That is my deeply held belief and it is the belief shared by the vast majority of the American people . . . A strong secure Israel is not just in Israel's interest. It's in the interest of the United States and in the interest of the entire free world.

Ronald Reagan: Only by full appreciation of the critical role the State of Israel plays in our strategic calculus can we build the foundation for thwarting Moscow's designs on territories and resources vital to our security and our national well-being.

Since the rebirth of the State of Israel, there has been an ironclad bond between that democracy and this one.

In Israel, free men and women are every day demonstrating the power of courage and faith. Back in 1948 when Israel was founded, pundits claimed the new country could never survive. Today, no one questions that Israel is a land of stability and democracy in a region of tyranny and unrest.

George Bush: The friendship, the alliance between the United States and Israel is strong and solid, built upon a foundation of shared democratic values, of shared history and heritage, that sustains the life of our two countries. The emotional bond of our people transcends politics. Our strategic cooperation—and I renew today our determination that that go forward—is a source of mutual security. And the United States' commitment to the security of Israel remains unshakeable. We may differ over some policies from time to time, individual policies, but never over the principle.

For more than forty years, the United States and Israel have enjoyed a friendship built on mutual respect and commitment to democratic principles. Our continuing search for peace in the Middle East begins with a recognition that the ties uniting our two countries can never be broken.

Bill Clinton: Our relationship would never vary from its allegiance to the shared values, the shared religious heritage, the shared democratic politics which have made the relationship between the United States and Israel a special—even on occasion a wonderful—relationship.

The United States admires Israel for all that it has overcome and for all that it has accomplished. We are proud of the strong bond we have forged with

Israel, based on our shared values and ideals. That unique relationship will endure just as Israel has endured. *(From a letter to Israeli Prime Minister Netanyahu on occasion of Israel's 50th birthday.)*

America and Israel share a special bond. Our relations are unique among all nations. Like America, Israel is a strong democracy, as a symbol of freedom, and an oasis of liberty, a home to the oppressed and persecuted.

The relationship between our two countries is built on shared understandings and values. Our peoples continue to enjoy the fruits of our excellent economic and cultural cooperation as we prepare to enter the 21st century. *(Clinton's reply after Israeli Ambassador Shoval presented his credentials, September 10, 1998)*

The point in all this is to highlight the union of nations, whether spiritually, democratically, economically, or militarily, there is a dramatic parallel between the rise of America to power and the simultaneous birth and rise of Israel to its destiny as well.

History of the Motto
"In God We Trust"

The motto *In God We Trust* was placed on United States coins largely because of the increased religious sentiment existing during the Civil War. Secretary of the Treasury Salmon P. Chase received many appeals from devout persons throughout the country, urging that the United States recognize the Deity on United States coins. From Treasury Department records, it appears that the first such appeal came in a letter dated November 13, 1861. It was written to Secretary Chase by Rev. M. R. Watkinson, Minister of the Gospel from Ridleyville, Penn., and read:

> Dear Sir: You are about to submit your annual report to the Congress respecting the affairs of the national finances.
>
> One fact touching our currency has hitherto been seriously overlooked. I mean the recognition of the Almighty God in some form on our coins.
>
> You are probably a Christian. What if our Republic were not shattered beyond reconstruction? Would not the antiquaries of succeeding centuries rightly reason from our past that we were a heathen nation? What I propose is that instead of the goddess of liberty we shall have next inside the 13 stars a ring inscribed with the words *Perpetual Union*; within the ring the all-seeing eye, crowned with a halo; beneath this eye the American flag, bearing in its field stars equal to the number of the States united; in the folds of the bars the words *God, Liberty, Law*.
>
> This would make a beautiful coin, to which no possible citizen could object. This would relieve us from the ignominy of heathenism. This would place us openly under the Divine protection we have personally claimed. From my hearth I have felt our national shame in disowning God as not the least of our present national disasters.
>
> To you first I address a subject that must be agitated.

As a result, Secretary Chase instructed James Pollock, Director of the Mint at Philadelphia, to prepare a motto, in a letter dated November 20, 1861:

Dear Sir: No nation can be strong except in the strength of God, or safe except in His defense. The trust of our people in God should be declared on our national coins.

You will cause a device to be prepared without unnecessary delay with a motto expressing in the fewest and tersest words possible this national recognition.

It was found that the Act of Congress dated January 18, 1837, prescribed the mottoes and devices that should be placed upon the coins of the United States. This meant that the mint could make no changes without the enactment of additional legislation by the Congress.

In December 1863, the Director of the Mint submitted designs for a new one-cent coin, two-cent coin, and three-cent coin to Secretary Chase for approval. He proposed that upon the designs either *Our Country*; *Our God* or *God, Our Trust* should appear as a motto on the coins.

In a letter to the Mint Director on December 9, 1863, Secretary Chase stated:

I approve your mottoes, only suggesting that on that with the Washington obverse the motto should begin with the word *Our*, so as to read *Our God and Our Country*. And on that with the shield, it should be changed so as to read: *In God We Trust*.

The Congress passed the Act of April 22, 1864. This legislation changed the composition of the one-cent coin and authorized the minting of the two-cent coin. The Mint Director was told to develop the designs for these coins for final approval of the Secretary. *In God We Trust* first appeared on the 1864 two-cent coin.

Another Act of Congress passed on March 3, 1865. It allowed the Mint Director, with the Secretary's approval, to place the motto on all gold and silver coins that "shall admit the inscription thereon." Under the Act, the motto was placed on the gold double-eagle coin, the gold eagle coin, and the gold half-eagle coin. It was also placed on the silver dollar coin, the half-dollar coin and the quarter-dollar coin, and on the nickel five-cent coin beginning in 1866. Later, Congress passed the Coinage Act of February 12, 1873. It also said that the Secretary "may cause the motto *In God We Trust* to be inscribed on such coins as shall admit of such motto."

The use of *In God We Trust* has not been uninterrupted. The motto disappeared from the five-cent coin in 1883, and did not reappear until production of the Jefferson nickel began in 1938.

Since 1938, all United States coins bear the inscription. Later, the motto was found missing from the new design of the double-eagle gold coin and the eagle gold coin shortly after they appeared in 1907. In response to a general demand, Congress ordered it restored, and the Act of May 18, 1908, made it mandatory on all coins upon which it had previously appeared. *In God We Trust* was not mandatory on the one-cent coin and five-cent coin. It could be placed on them by the Secretary or the Mint Director with the Secretary's approval.

The motto has been in continuous use on the one-cent coin since 1909, and on the ten-cent coin since 1916. It also has appeared on all gold coins and silver dollar coins, half-dollar coins, and quarter-dollar coins struck since July 1, 1908.

A law was passed by the 84th Congress (P.L. 84–140) and approved by the President on July 11, 1955. It said that the motto should appear on all United States paper currency and coins. This law provides that:

> At such time as new dies for the printing of currency are adopted in connection with the current program of the Treasury Department to increase the capacity of presses utilized by the Bureau of Engraving and Printing, the dies shall bear, at such place or places thereon as the Secretary of the Treasury may determine to be appropriate, the inscription *In God We Trust,* and thereafter this inscription shall appear on all United States currency and coins.

On July 30, 1956, the President approved a Joint Resolution of the 84th Congress, declaring *In God We Trust* the national motto of the United States. *In God We Trust* was first used on paper money in 1957, when it appeared on the one-dollar silver certificate. The first paper currency bearing the motto entered circulation on October 1, 1957. The Bureau of Engraving and Printing (BEP) was converting to the dry intaglio printing process. During this conversion, it gradually included *In God We Trust* in the back design of all classes and denominations of currency.

A Recent Testimony
to the Power of Love

This praise report reflects the love of Christ displayed at the Marilyn Manson concert held on April 28, 1999, in Cedar Rapids, Iowa—the final concert of his tour.

Manson's music had been associated with the Littleton tragedy, making the climate ripe for a potentially anger-driven reaction. In fact, a local movement had begun to picket, protest, and petition in opposition to the concert. The police, the media, and the community were prepared for angry protests and ugly brawling between Christians and Manson supporters. The outlook was grim.

But many faithful believers had been fervently praying for four weeks that God would be glorified in this volatile situation. God was about to answer their prayers.

Suddenly, something totally unexpected happened. Emerging through the vehicle of e-mail, another local movement suddenly sprang to life—that the only way to truly change our moral climate is to soften hard hearts (the hearts of Manson fans have been hardened by their perception that Christians are mean-spirited, hateful, and judgmental). The idea was birthed to unravel that stereotype by Christians showing the love of Christ to these fans in tangible ways.

This approach apparently touched many, as e-mails were forwarded to hundreds of people all over the city and across the country. Scores of people affirmed this loving approach and pledged their prayer support. Creative ideas began formulating in churches across the city. Yet, everyone wondered what was about to happen.

Concert day arrived and tension filled the community. Some fans had actually expressed being fearful of going downtown because of what the "Christian freaks" might do to hurt or harass them. The media geared up for an ugly battle between Manson fans and the Christian "opposition."

Instead, as reported in the C.R. Gazette the next day: "While the Five Seasons Center hired extra security outside in anticipation of demonstrators, no one held signs opposing the concert."

How unbelievable this is, in light of the Littleton incident! A previous night's concert had seen "hundreds of demonstrators rally outside a Manson concert . . . protesting possible links between his dark music and the Colorado school killings" (AP News).

But what was seen in Cedar Rapids was an amazing testament to the power and love of Christ! Scores of Christians from churches in eastern Iowa converged on the sidewalks outside the Five Seasons Center to do two positive things: pray and show unmistakable love. It was a sight to behold.

AS FOR PRAYER:

~Over 40 people met at the Father's House, a downtown church, for intercessory prayer and worship—people from over a dozen churches were represented.

~Groups conducted "prayer walks" around the Five Seasons Center. People prayed in huddles on the sidewalk. Churches around the city and youth groups held special prayer meetings.

~People all over the U.S. were praying (in Washington, Texas, Oklahoma, Missouri, Michigan, and across Iowa).

~As many as twenty pastors and Christian leaders actually went into the concert arena to pray specifically during the concert for God's protection from destructive messages and for the salvation of those trapped by the darkness. They mostly prayed in pairs around the stadium—and at one point many of them came together in a visible display of united, concerted prayer.

AS FOR SHOWING LOVE TO THE FANS:

~While the concert goers waited to get into the Five Seasons Center, they were treated to pizza, soda, juice, cookies, and sandwiches. All was given away in the name of the Lord, with a smile and no strings attached. Acts of kindness just overwhelmed the kids.

~The media, the fans, the Five Seasons staff, the police and even Manson's crew took notice. One of our pastors was interviewed by the Gazette and said, "We want the kids here to know not all Christians are judgmental or hate-mongers. Our desire is . . . to reach out to them with the love of Christ and to let them know we care."

~One pastor asked Manson fans how he could pray for them—about twenty shared specific needs and were prayed for.

~After the concert, about $200 in cash (collected mostly by a local youth group) was given out to pay for parking in the parking ramp. The Christians involved said, "We're Christians and we'd like to show you God's love by paying for your parking tonight." With one exception, every carload gratefully accepted it. What a final impression of the night!

RESULTS OF THIS LOVE IN ACTION:

People asked, "Why are you doing this?" and then listened to the answer. Faces of fans looked surprised as they approached the area, expecting conflict but finding love instead. The police had pleasant encounters with the Christians. Parents dropping off their kids at the concert saw love being shown their children. Many people engaged fans in positive, non-judgmental conversations. After receiving the pizza, one kid commented, "Wow, Marilyn Manson never gave me anything!"

As for the concert itself, we saw God work a miracle. After only an hour, Manson abruptly ended the concert early. During his "nazi/antichrist" stage set, he flew into a rage and stormed off the stage, never to return! A Christian policeman reported that he then proceeded to destroy his dressing room. Everyone in the audience looked around, puzzled by what they had just witnessed. The crowd shouted, "Manson, Manson, Manson," but he never returned.

In summary, the entire city was touched by the love of Jesus; the news media, the police, the superintendent of schools and thousands of parents and students had a revelation of Christ's mercy. Indeed, many fans came to the concert convinced that Christians were irritating and that Marilyn Manson was impressive; many left the concert feeling that Marilyn Manson was irritating and that Christians were impressive! Think of how much closer to the kingdom these kids may be as a result of this outreach event.

We pray that Marilyn Manson will find true peace for his troubled soul, which only comes through knowing Jesus Christ. Like so many of his fans, he is searching frantically for fulfillment—but unfortunately in all the wrong places. We trust that the "free gifts" of love that we gave through words and actions may have brought Marilyn and his fans at least a step closer to finding the one "Free Gift" that Jesus has to offer.

Marilyn Manson's visit here brought the body of Christ together in unprecedented ways and gave us visible proof of the power of love and prayer. A number of city officials were touched by the demonstration of love from the church. May other communities learn from our experience.

—compiled by Mark Forstrom, youth pastor
New Covenant Church, Cedar Rapids, IA

Praying for America
10-tape album

Now that you have read this message, you can also listen to these teachings as they were first presented by Francis Frangipane. Choose your favorites for $4:00 each or enjoy the entire 10-tape album for just $37.50.

1.	A World Without America	#PA01
2.	Mercy Triumphs Over Judgment	#PA02
3.	What Are You Becoming?	#PA03
4.	One Man	#PA04
5.	Prayer Changes the Mind of God	#PA05
6.	Pardon for an Unrepentant People	#PA06
7.	God Talking to God	#PA07
8.	The Beloved	#PA08
9.	He Will Sprinkle Many Nations	#PA09
10.	America Awakened to God's Highest Purpose	#PA10

To place order, call 319-395-7833. Individual tapes are $4.00 each (plus S/H). The 10-tape album, #1FF5-039, is $37.50 (plus S/H).

River of Life Newsletter

The first two chapters from this book were printed in the River of Life newsletter, February 1999. We've had many requests for that issue. For bulk copies of that issue, 10-99 copies are .22 each, 100-499 are .20 each, and 500+ are .15 each. Call 1-319-395-7833 to place your order.

In Christ's Image

Television Ministry

Francis Frangipane is on the Angel One channel on the Dominion Sky Angel satellite system, 9 p.m. EST Fridays and 11 a.m. EST Wednesdays.

Radio Ministry

A one-half hour daily radio program by Francis is now on the air. Call 1-888-934-6243 for updated listings of radio stations and times for your locale.

Internet Ministries

http://www.InChristsImage.org for teachings on audio and video
http://www.Frangipane.org for current articles and other resources